Marinka

From Havana to Burlesque

The Autobiography of
Marinka
'Queen of the Amazons'

by
Marinka Melanie Hunter
&
Lily Star

Contents

Preface

Chapters

1 - Havana (September 23, 1959)   3
2 - My Family   13
3 - Nefertiti, Baby and Bruno   25
4 - Armando   27
5 - The Powderpuff Revue   35
6 - Bobby Colt   55
7 - Meeting Rod   61
8 - Mixing Clubs   67
9 - Dr. Prado   73
10 - The Follies Burlesk   77
11 - Sex Change Operation   81
12 - Becoming a Burlesque Feature   111
13 - The Catskills   115
14 - Married to Rod   119
15 - Playing the Field   143
16 - Switzerland   149
17 - Meeting Tony   155
18 - All That Jazz   165
19 - Returning to Switzerland   169
20 - Union City, New Jersey   179
21 - Meeting Bobby   183
22 - On the Road Again   193

Preface

    I want to tell my story for people to both enjoy and to also learn who I am. I am not just a woman wearing makeup, beads and feathers. Inside is a human full of emotions and concerns for others. My empathy for people who feel like me is the force that pushed me to write this book. I am at the end of my life and feel it is the perfect time. If I had done this when I was 30, it would have been a sensation instead of my story.

I want to apologize to the people I've known over the years and to those who are still my friends who did not know about the skeleton in my closet. It was never my intention to fool anyone. We all have secrets in our hearts that belong to us. I truly want my friends who never knew that I was born different, to know that I am the same person and I love them. The decision to "tell all" was not easy. But I want to live the rest of my life at peace, no longer having to quiet the voice that has always wanted to cry out!

Chapter 1 - Havana (September 23, 1959)

In the Havana airport, Rancho Boyeros, I hugged and kissed my father knowing that it would be the last day I would see him alive. With us was my mother, my sister, Francis, and my nephew, Norberto. My sister, Micaela, her husband Carlos and their children, Diana and Carlos were also there to see me off. The announcement for the departure of my flight to New York came over the air. It was time. I hugged all my family and with tears in my eyes I went back and hugged my father again. We were both crying as I walked away. I had one piece of luggage and two thousand dollars in one hundred-dollar bills. As I approached the check point and saw the police, I was afraid that they would take my money. When they asked how much money I had, I declared the two thousand dollars. When they asked me why I was going to New York, I told them I was going to study English. I was relieved when they returned my passport and boarding pass. This was Castro's Cuba!

When the communist party came to power, Havana's music, nightlife, culture and entertainment no longer existed, and democracy was gone. In its place was a military state, where every human right was being violated. Life was cheap. The sounds of firing squads could be heard day and night. All the cadets of the military city, Columbia, were killed and replaced with men with long hair ready to kill in the name of "The Revolution". It was a common practice to round up anyone suspected of being a Batista sympathizer and send them to a firing squad.

Inside the plane, for four hours I was lost in thought. I was worried about leaving my family in Havana and unsure of what the future held for me in New York. I felt guilty for leaving my father when he needed me the most. I thought if I could have got out of the plane, I would have stayed with him and with my poor mother who was

3

devastated and in tears as I walked away. I awoke from my thoughts to hear the pilot announcing that we would be landing at New York International Airport.

I walked to immigration and handed the officer a manila envelope with all my documents from the American Embassy in Cuba along with my passport. He looked over the documents, gave me a form to sign, stamped my passport "Resident", and gave me the address to the immigration department. He told me that if I did not receive my green card in two weeks, that I needed to go to that address. I walked out and met my godmother, Irene, my godfather, Idelphonso, and their son, Alphonso. We hugged and gave greetings. I followed them to the bus to Kew Garden Station, where we picked up the elevated subway to their home in Manhattan. This was the first time that I had ever seen skyscrapers. They seemed to be so powerful and I was completely overwhelmed.

My family lived on Broadway and 137th St. in a three-bedroom apartment. That evening, a few of their close friends came to meet me and we had hors d'ouvres and wine. Everyone kept asking me about the political situation in Cuba. Among my godmother's friends, the most interesting to me was a lady named Sarita and her son William. Sarita was my nephew Alphonso's godmother. She was a tall blonde beautiful lady. We became best friends. She was always there to help guide me and help navigate my way through my new life in New York.

The next morning, my godfather took me to midtown Manhattan to get my social security card. Then he took me shopping at Macy's. I was fascinated with the volume of inventory in the stores. I purchased undergarments, shoes, some sweaters and a winter coat. We went to lunch and I had my very first hamburger, french fries and a coke. After lunch, we walked a few blocks to the New York garment center. My godmother / sister, Irene, worked there as a sample maker. Irene introduced me to all the people in the showroom as her younger brother. I was fascinated by the models and the dresses. To me it

4

was like a fantasy land, and I loved that everyone adored Irene.

Irene was my mother's fifth child, but she was the third child to survive. I was number thirteen and when I was born, Irene was already sixteen years old and engaged to Idelphonso. Prior to my birth my mother had seven more children. Only four survived infancy. Six years after my sister Mercedes was born, she became pregnant with me. When I was born my sister, Irene, was so excited to have a new little brother. That was the beginning of her love for me. She asked my mother if she could stand as my godmother at my baptismal.

A few days later, my godfather came home with good news. The foreman in the leather and fur garment factory where he worked was looking for someone to cut and trim the leather garments to be cleaned for the next step in production. I was paid $1.00/ hr. which was the minimum wage in New York City in 1959. I was so happy to have a job even at thirty-five dollars per week. This was still a lot of money as I didn't have to pay for room and board. The only thing my godfather asked of me was that I open a bank account and deposit ten dollars per week from my paycheck. He was teaching me how to save money and be prepared for my future as they had saved enough money in three years to make a down payment on a home.

I had never had a job before going to work in the factory. This was all very new to me. I quickly learned all my responsibilities and before I knew it, I was making friends. My godfather was always keeping an eye on me. When we left the factory at 4pm each day, he would tell me, "Don't get too friendly with the people that you work with."

One day during my break, I met a good-looking boy named Hector. He was around my age and worked part time in the office while attending college. He had been born and raised in New York City and was much more streetwise than me. He wasn't as tall as I was, but he was very strong and had a great body. His eyes were the most beautiful green eyes I had ever seen. 5

Hector asked me if I would like to meet him on Saturday night and he would show me the New York that I did not know. I told him I would like that, but I would have to ask my godmother for permission. Irene told me I could go with him, but I needed to be home by eleven and that I could not drink.

That Saturday I took the subway to 72nd St. and Broadway. I met Hector in the Horn and Hardart Automat Cafeteria. Automat cafeterias were very popular then. You changed your money to coin and placed the coins in a slot that then allowed you to open the window and remove your selection. They offered a variety of food such as chicken pot pie, Boston beans, sandwiches, and pies. We both bought a coffee and sat down at a table. Hector asked me if I was gay. I told him that I did not know what gay meant. He explained that it was when a boy likes another boy. So, I asked him if he was gay. He replied, "Yes I am." I told him, "I must be because I like you."

When our coffees were finished, he asked if I would like to go to a gay bar. While walking to the bar, Hector asked me if I had ever been to bed with another boy. I told him that I had never been to bed with a boy or a girl but that I had a horrible rape experience and I did not really want to talk about it.

Before I knew it, we arrived at the 77 Club, but they wouldn't let me in because I didn't bring my passport and had not yet received my green card. Hector said he would call some friends and see if any of them were having a house party. There was a party, and we needed to buy a six pack of beer for admission to the party. We bought the beer and walked a few blocks to an apartment building. Hector announced himself over the intercom, the door unlocked, and we went upstairs. Once we were inside the apartment, I could not believe my eyes. It was full of boys dancing with each other. The host was all made up like a girl and introduced himself as Carmela. I was completely mesmerized by so many boys dancing with each other. I could not have ever imagined a situation like that. Carmela gave us a beer; the music was loud, and I

6

recognized some of the songs. They played "Chances Are" by Johnny Mathis and Hector asked me to dance.

It was nearing eleven o'clock and I told Hector that I needed to go home. He walked with me to the 79th and Broadway subway station. Hector hugged me and kissed me on the lips. He said, "I'll see you, Monday." While riding the train home, all I could think was, "How wonderful is New York?" I had a job, I found out I was gay, I had been to my first gay party and I had a man who was crazy about me.

The next day, Hector called me. We couldn't say much to each other because my entire family was with me in the room. He asked me to go outside and call him on his private line. So, I went out to the candy store and called him. He romanced me over the phone. It felt like I was in paradise as I had never had a romantic experience like this. He asked to meet again the following Saturday. He told me he would have the house to himself as his family would be out of town. He wanted to know if I could stay with him. I told him I would need to ask Irene for permission and would let him know when I saw him on Monday.

That Sunday afternoon as usual we called Havana to talk to my parents and to find out how my father was doing. I was nineteen years old, but I remember having a conversation with my father and promising him two things. He asked that I always look after my mother once he was gone and to obey the wishes of my godparents while I was living with them in New York.

That evening, in my room, I thought about how nice Hector was and wondered if he would ask me for sex if I went to his home the following weekend. The thought of sex terrified me as just a few months before in Havana, when my mother asked me to go to the grocery store, I walked out of the building where we lived and there were two jeeps full of Castro's soldiers. They were looking for someone and asked me if I knew them. I told them that we had just recently moved into the building and that I did not know the person they were asking about. One of

the soldiers took me by the hand and asked me to follow
him. He took me across the street to a building that had
been damaged during the revolution. Behind the stairs
he forced me to take down my pants. He then proceeded
to brutally sodomize me. When he was finished, he
whispered in my ear and told me to stay there for awhile
and not to come out. Then he walked away. Being
confused, depressed, violated and in pain, I cannot say
how long I stayed there behind the stairs.

After a while I just slowly walked back home. When
my mother saw me, she asked what happened and where
the groceries were. I just told her that there were too
many soldiers and I was afraid to walk to the store. I
took a shower and tried to compose myself. With my
father's illness and my mother having to deal with that, I
could not bring myself to tell her what happened to me.
Later that evening when my sister, Francis, came home,
I told her what happened. She told my mother not to let
me out of the house anymore and that she would get the
groceries.

That Sunday night, I asked Irene if I could spend the
following weekend with Hector at his home. Irene asked
my godfather, "Who is this Hector friend of Chacho's?"
Idelphonso told her he was a good boy who worked in the
factory office. Irene told me that it was okay for me to go.

When Friday came, I took a little bag with a change
of clothes and my toiletries. When I arrived at Hector's,
I rang the bell. He answered from upstairs and told me
to come on up. As I climbed the stairs, I looked up to
see Hector. He was standing in the doorway shirtless
and striking a pose. He put his arms around me and
started to kiss me. I was terrified. Hector asked me why
I was shaking. I told him that I was afraid because his
affection was new to me and reminded me of my horrible
experience in Havana.

Hector hugged me and very sweetly told me not to
worry. He said that he understood that it was my first
time and that he would be gentle, all the while he was
undressing me. Before I knew it, we were in his bed

8

making love. When we were finished, I went to take a shower. In the mirror I could see bruises on my shoulders and neck. I showed the bruises to Hector. I said, "Look what you did to me." He said, "Oh baby you make me crazy." I asked him how I was supposed to explain it to my family. He told me to tell them the truth. He said that my family must know that I was gay, just by looking at me.

We talked a little while over a dish of ice cream. Hector said that we needed to go out and celebrate. When I asked what the occasion was, he replied "Us." We got dressed and headed out to the gay bar. This time I had my green card. Hector said 'We are coming together, and we are leaving together. If anybody says anything, tell them you are mine. This is your first time in a gay bar so try to stay next to me." We arrived at the 77 Club on 77th and Broadway. This time they let me right in.

The 77 Club had an enormous bar that covered the entire right side of the room. The left side of the club had tables and chairs. Against the left wall stood a huge juke box. Hector bought us both a beer. The juke box started to play one of my favorite songs, "Only You", by The Platters. Hector told me that he would like to dance with me, but dancing was not allowed in the 77 Club.

A tall slender man entered the club. His face was completely made up and his right arm was covered in gorgeous bangles. He was a queen in every sense of the word. He approached us and immediately hugged Hector. Hector introduced him to me as Nefertiti. I could not believe my ears and wanted to ask him questions, but I was too shy. He walked away to greet other friends. Later he asked us to join him at a table. He instantaneously asked me, "Who are you? Where are you from? How old are you?" We laughed and had a fabulous time. Nefertiti mentioned that he was working on his gown to wear to a ball. He gave me his number of which Hector was fine with and said that he wanted me to meet Ninon. At the end of the evening we went back to Hector's and went to sleep.

Hector and I spent the next day going to Central Park

and Greenwich Village. We had lunch in the village. I asked Hector, "What is this ball that Nefertiti mentioned?" He told me that it was forbidden for men to dress in women's clothes in public. At special times of the year, like Halloween, Thanksgiving, Valentines Day, etc., there were celebrations held where men could dress in drag without worrying about being arrested. The drag queens would take this opportunity to go to the balls looking like movie stars. When I heard this, all I could think was how badly I wanted to participate.

We went to a gay bar, Julius' Bar, in The Village. Hector had a friend who tended bar there. We had a beer and later went to dinner at Tads Steakhouse. It was late so we headed back to Hector's so I could gather my belongings and head back to my home.

The following Wednesday, I called Nefertiti. He invited me to stop by on Friday. I went to his house and that is when I met Ninon. I was enchanted by Ninon. He named himself after Ninon Sevilla, a Cuban Rumbera who was famous in the Mexican films. We were both very effeminate and after talking I found out that we had similar interests and goals. We became very close.

Nefertiti and Ninon were working on their gowns to wear to the Artists' Exotic Halloween Carnival and Ball. This annual event was to be held at the Manhattan Center. There was one very peculiar thing about Nefertiti's home and that was Delilah, the four-foot-long ocelot. Nefertiti offered to lend me a costume if I wanted to go to the ball. I was not prepared to attend as it was only one week away. Nefertiti told me that if I wore a jacket and a tie, I could escort Ninon and Hector could escort Nefertiti. I called Hector to ask if he was interested. He said, "Yes".

Halloween night, we met at Nefertiti's and escorted Nefertiti and Ninon to the Manhattan Center. When we arrived in our taxi, I couldn't believe the spectacle. The police were directing traffic, there were people all through the streets with cameras and the media was photographing all the drag queens. The drag queens would exit their vehicles and parade and pose like they were going to the Oscars. They looked like movie stars and these balls were a huge event.

Most of the people who attended were straight and dressed to the nines. Reservations were necessary and tickets were sold months in advance. They were very expensive for the time at $75 to $100 per ticket. Some people dressed in gowns and some wore show girl outfits. It was like a huge masquerade ball filled with costumes that had been thought out and put together just for this event. At the end of the evening, they had a contest and gave awards for best costume, most beautiful and best gown. The contests always closed out the ball. The international press was there to photograph the event. You would find photos months later in different publications of people attending the ball. This was only my second month in New York and I already felt like I belonged there.

Chapter 2 - My Family

I was born in Palma Soriano, Oriente, Cuba on the 6th of January, on my mother's 38th birthday. I consider this my natal birth. My actual birth occurred many years later in New York.

My father, Jose Arias, and my mother, Maria Moreno, Rodriquez were both originally from Spain. My mother was born in Seville in southern Spain on January 6, 1902. My father was born in Santa Maria De Go, in Lugo Galicia in northwest Spain on March 17, 1895. Galicia and Seville were not only separated by geography but also in their histories, cultures and weather.

My maternal grandmother, Maria Rodriquez Espinosa, was widowed at a very young age and left alone to raise my mother. Because she was from Triana, which is the neighborhood in Seville where flamenco was born, she was quite accustomed to dancing Sevillanas. When my grandfather died, she used her dancing skills to perform flamenco in order to support herself and my mother. She was hired to perform on a cruise ship that travelled from Cadiz to Havana. As she couldn't always take my mother with her, she would often leave her with the local nuns. My mother received most of her education from the nuns. They not only taught the girls to read and write but also prepared them to be wives and mothers.

While working on the cruise ship, my grandmother met a wealthy Spanish man named Ramon Otero, who wanted to marry her. She took Maria on the next cruise to meet her would be stepfather. Once my grandmother was married, she and my mother moved to live in Santiago de Cuba.

Ramon Otero was a man from Madrid who emigrated to Santiago de Cuba when Cuba was part of Spain, where he made his fortune. He was the president of the Power Company of Santiago de Cuba and the owner of the Firmesa Mines.

My father was a well-educated young man. His reasons for going to Cuba were much different than those of my mother. His father was the priest of the only church in Santa Maria de Go. His mother had a life-long relationship with this priest and had two children with him, my father and my aunt. However, no one questioned this as it would be customary for a priest to assist a single mother with two children. As an adult my father found out the truth about who is father was.

He had always been told his father had died but after realizing there was no paternal name on his birth certificate, he knew the rumors were true. He went to the priest and his mother and asked for the truth. They responded that he needed to go to Cuba to live with his Uncle Manuel. Uncle Manuel worked at the Spanish Embassy in Santiago de Cuba. Uncle Manuel not only received my father but got him a job at the embassy.

After a few months of living in Santiago de Cuba, my grandparents hosted a Christmas party. They invited the deacon of Santiago Cathedral. He invited his friend, Jose. My mother was 19 and when she and Jose met, they felt an immediate attraction. After an eleven-month courtship, they were married in El Caney on November 6, 1922.

Following the wedding my father went to work for his father in law, Ramon Otero. Since my father was educated in engineering, he fit in well working at Ramon's Firmesa Mines.

In 1925, my father met an American, Mr. Smith, who owned four sugar refineries throughout the Oriente Province. Mr. Smith was very impressed with my father's education and work experience, so he asked my father to be the director of his sugar refineries. My father worked for Mr. Smith until he retired in 1958.

My mother, Maria, was a wife and mother. She had a total of thirteen children. She birthed four boys and nine girls which included two sets of twins. Only eight of her children lived to adulthood; three died of influenza, and two died from diptheria. In 1940, I, the last child, was born into a household of six sisters and one brother.

My father gave me the name Humberto Arias Moreno. My older siblings had already been married and moved out of the house. It had been six years since my mother had my sister, Mercedes. Mercedes was six and my sister, Manuela, was eight. Along with my sisters and parents I also had a nanny, Panchita. I was very close with my mother and Panchita. They were always there for me and kept a very watchful eye. I was closest to Mercedes and treated as the "baby" of the family. I was the thirteenth child and born on the Catholic Feast of the Epiphany. It is celebrated on the thirteenth night after Christmas Eve and it commemorates the arrival of the Three Kings.

As a young child, my family noticed that I was different from other boys and my siblings just considered me another one of the girls. My parents took me to a fair when I was five. I was thrilled with the merry go round. I had my first cotton candy and visited a Spanish Gypsy fortuneteller. I remember her speaking with my mother and my mother paying her some money. Years later my mother told me that the fortuneteller had told her that I was "Born under a star, a different star".

As the youngest and only five at the time, I was at home while my older siblings were at school. I would often put on my sisters' clothes and parade around the house to entertain Panchita and my mother. They would laugh and tell me that I better be careful as my sisters would be mad if they knew. One time I went into my mother's chest of drawers because I wanted to try on her stockings. I put on my sister's shoes, walked out to show off as I often did, unaware that my father was home as well. There I was walking around holding up my mother's expensive silk stockings with my fingers and wearing her bloomers and my sister's shoes. My main audience, Panchita, was over in the corner laughing as usual. Stockings were a must for women to wear and were in great shortage due to World War II. I can only recall a few times that my parents felt the need to punish me. This was one of them. My mother pushed me on my butt all the way back to her room. She took the clothes off me and sent me to my room for the rest of the day.

My mother never cared for Cuba. She hated the heat and the hurricanes. She passed the time creating a warm and loving household. My mother was a good cook and liked to cook Spanish cuisine. I can vividly recall the taste of her garbanzo bean and chorizo soup. She also liked to have red wine with dinner. I can't remember how old I was when I first started to drink wine, but I know I was young and still to this day enjoy red wine with dinner. She also loved to do needlework and listen to her favorite radio show, "The Right to Be Born", which eventually became a film. I would sit with her and listen as well. She also allowed us to have multiple pets. We had German Shepherds, a parrot named Pepe, a three-legged alley cat named Tres Patines among others. We had a very relaxed household, my mother taught us to pray when we awoke in the morning and pray at night before bedtime. We were catholic and attended mass every Sunday.

I was generally a healthy child though I did suffer from bouts of anemia. I did not like to eat meat. I felt sorry that they had to kill the animals. I would hide the meat in my napkin and throw it away. To remedy my lack of iron, my mother would give me a concoction of duck egg yolk and sherry wine. I had to drink this remedy every morning for several months. Other than that, I was rarely ill.

I was six years old when I entered school. I liked music classes. I was good at grammar and loved to read and still do. I did not like physical education. I would get panic attacks. My mother asked the school not to put me in those classes. It was apparent to everyone, that I was an unusual child. I spent a lot of time by myself and felt alienated. Playing with the boys did not appeal to me. The boys would tease me and call me names and often bullied and beat me for being different. I came home sad and depressed every day.

My sister Mercedes and I would play together a lot. I loved rainy days, because we could stay inside and play. She would show me how to dress her dolls and other girl stuff. I would get so upset when my sister wouldn't let me

16

play with her dolls.

When I was seven, I was given a pair of guns, a cowboy hat, and boys' trucks for Christmas. I started to cry because I wanted the dolls that my sister received. I think that was the moment that my parents truly realized that there was something different about me. Even today, I love collecting dolls. I think it's because I was denied as a child.

My father had a small library in his office. My family was always reading books and listening to the radio novellas. Because my mother saw how I was, she had me read the lives of the saints from St. Augustine to Santa Teresa de Jesus. At seven years old, I became obsessed with these saints.

When I was about eight years old, the school principal called my mother. His complaint was that I was "different" from the other children. He told my mother that my mannerisms were too effeminate. My teacher would often lecture me and hit me with books to drive his point home. The other boys would react to me because I was different and cause a commotion. But I was always blamed for it. One of my teachers even tried to teach me how to walk more like a man.

My family moved to Holguin, Cuba in 1949. They rented a house, near La Loma De La Cruz, the Hill of the Cross, near Holguin College. I attended the Pedagogico Institute Academy, which was a very expensive private all-boys school. Most of the boys there also made fun of me and called me many derogatory names, but the one I remember the most was "Galleguito Pajarito". It means Galician bird. I know it sounds innocent enough, but it was extremely offensive for a boy at the time. Cubans refer to gay men as pajaros. {Birds} I did make one friend who would protect me from the other boys. His name was Oscar Asset. He was five years older than I was and my mother never approved of this friendship.

Even though we missed our home in Marcane, I liked Holguin. It was beautiful. We later built a new home in Reparto Llenin in the suburbs of Holguin. It was an upscale development with a golf and country club. I liked it there and it wasn't too far from the Marcane Sugar Refinery, where my father worked. The refinery was later renamed Loinaz Echevarria, after the founder of the communist party in Cuba.

The sugar cane plantations in Biran belonged to Fidel Castro's father, Angel. He was also Galician and therefore enjoyed a close relationship with my father. They spoke to one another in their native language. No one could ever understand what they were saying. The Cuban people referred to the Spaniards as "Gallego", since most of them were from Galicia.

Every year, my father would order cases of Cardenal Mendoza, his favorite Spanish brandy. Angel's wife, Lina Ruz Gonzalez, would come over to drink brandy with my father while doing business. This was because Angel was illiterate, so Lina helped him with writing and running the business. It was required that my father do business with her, since they provided the sugar cane to the refinery.

Lina was the daughter of Angel Castro's cook. They were married when she was quite young. She became a mother to five of the Castro children. Fidel's older brother, Ramon Eusebio Castro Ruz, wanted to marry my sister/godmother, Irene. The Castro families were very friendly and sociable.

The Martinez family was another Gallego family who were friends of my parents. They had three boys, Alfonso, Juan, and Pablo. I went to their house to play and all of us boys were talking out in the garden. The other boys wanted to climb a big tree in the backyard. I told them I didn't want to, but they picked me up and swung me in the air. I fell to the ground, hurt, and crying. I couldn't even get up on my own. Mrs. Martinez ordered her sons to bring me into the house and she called my mother. My mother, along with Panchita, came to get me and took me to the emergency room. I was in bed for two weeks recovering from my injuries. After that incident, I was not allowed to play at a friend's house. If my friends wanted to play, they had to come to mine.

Mario, my favorite nephew, used to come to visit often. He was my parent's first grandchild. He took after my father and my older brother Antonio. He was an Arias in every sense of the name. He learned a lot of skills from my father many of which I had no interest. The one thing that bothered me was that my father would sit and teach Mario the Galician language. I would have loved to learn and spend this time with my father but because my interests were so different from his, we didn't spend much time together. I can only assume that he thought I wasn't interested. After many more grandchildren were born, Mario remained my father's favorite.

Mario was six years younger than me, but we still had a lot in common. We spent quite a bit of time together swimming in the river, bird watching, and going to see movies. He was a real friend and like a brother to me. I have very fond memories of him. Even now, whenever we are in touch, we still enjoy reminiscing over our childhood memories.

My mother had always planned to return to Spain. She would often say that as soon as they could sell the house and farm, we would go. My mother wanted to move to Seville and my father wanted to go back to Galicia. My father agreed to finally sell the house, but that we would be going to Galicia. My mother was still insisting upon going to Seville. My father eventually won the argument, however neither ever happened.

We left Holguin and went back to Palma Soriano. Palma Soriano was another sugar refinery city where my father conducted business. It was a large city with the biggest river in Cuba, Rio Cauto. It was this river that separated the city from the central azucarero, or sugar refinery. Near the refinery there was a complex known as the Herradura. It was beautifully landscaped and had multiple recreation areas. There were approximately sixteen houses in the Herradura which were all owned by the refinery. Only the owners and top executives could live there.

Cuba was a racist society, there was no mixing of the

races in any way. It wasn't a violent type of racism it was just a social way of life. Everyone went to his or her own social clubs. The Spanish stayed in La Colonia Espanola, The Fenix was for black Cubans and the Lyceum social clubs were for Cubans only.

When I was eleven my family went to a Carnivale ball in La Colonia Espanola. I stayed home with Panchita. When she went to sleep, I decided that I was going to the ball too. I went to my mother's room looking for something to wear, but none of her clothes fit me anymore. I could only use her jewelry and red lipstick. I remember this moment every time I wear red lipstick.

I went to my sisters' room and picked out different colored clothes and a pair of shoes that fit. I then proceeded to apply every color of eye shadow I could find and penciled my eyes in black. I wore my mother's mantilla. I used a silk orchid to keep it attached to my head. I looked in the mirror and thought that I was beautiful but realized that with all the colors I was wearing, I looked like a Spanish Gypsy.

After Panchita went to bed, I went out. I took off my shoes as to not make any noise. It was a few blocks to La Colonia Espanola. When I got there, I could hear the music playing inside and I headed into the hall. Eduardo, a young man I knew, was at the door. I greeted him by name, and he let me in. You could tell by the look on his face that he was perplexed as to who I was.

The band was playing a Paso Doble and Eduardo and a few other men wanted to dance with me. During one of the turns around the ballroom, I was facing the table where my family was seated. My mother instantly recognized me. The silk orchid of her Mantilla was a dead giveaway. She smiled at me and sent my godfather over. He said to me "Chacho, let's go home before your father and sisters recognize you." He scurried me out as if he was my escort. When we arrived back home, we made enough commotion to wake Panchita. She asked me, "When did you do all that, and where are you going?" I had to explain that I had been brought back from the ball.

She was laughing and completely surprised that I had pulled this off. She helped me clean my face and put me to bed.

In the morning, my mother came to wake me. She said, "Never again should you dare to do this." I had to spend the entire day in my room. My mother did not want to see me so Panchita brought me my dinner. I didn't mind being punished because I had so much fun that night.

One day in December 1952, when I came home from school, Panchita served me my snack as usual. My parents seemed to be fascinated with an article in the newspaper. When they were finished, they sat the paper on the kitchen table. I picked it up and saw on the front page a photo of a blonde woman and a small photo of a soldier. In large letters, it said, "Christine Jorgensen the American soldier that became a woman." I continued to read the entire article and then I told my mother that I wanted to be like Christine. She asked me what I was talking about. She sent Panchita to call for my father. When my father came to the room, my mother made me repeat for him what I had told her. My father's response was, "Take Chacho to see Dr. Silva."

Dr. Silva did a complete physical, he examined my entire body. He was trying to find the cause of what would make me desire to be a different sex. He concluded that I was healthy and normal and that there wasn't anything physically wrong with me.

My parents examined all my possessions in my room. They were looking to see if I had any books or magazines that could be the source of my desire. When they couldn't find anything, they called the priest. My parents felt like this was very unnatural and without any other explanation wanted the spiritual advice of the church. They took me to see Father Juan. After confession for about an hour, he told my parents that spiritually I was fine.

My mother arranged with Father Juan for me to go to study in the seminary, San Basilio El Magno in El Cobre. This was located right next to the Basilica of Our Lady of Charity, who was the patron virgin of Cuba. The seminary was very old and was of typical Spanish architecture. The cement was white, and the roof was red Spanish tiles. The entrance was a double hand-crafted wooden door with a small window that opened to enable one to see who was knocking. Above the door in bronze was "Seminario San Basilio El Magno". Just inside the doors was a beautiful garden with a statue of a monk in long robes. Off to the sides were the offices of the administration and rectory. Along the corridors were rooms for study. The first floor also included the infirmary, chapel, kitchen and dining room. The second floor is where the students showered and slept. Our rooms were called cells; they were very small and had two beds in each. The priests' rooms were also located on the second floor. We only went up there to sleep or shower.

In the seminary it was required to meet with the spiritual priest almost daily. It was his job to find out how I was feeling about my duties and the concept of becoming a priest. I studied Latin, theology and had to read a lot of books. We also had duties in the seminary and basilica. It was my daily duty to replace the flowers on the altar of the basilica and to keep it clean. My life was very peaceful, and I felt very good spiritually, but I was not content. After only a few months I knew I did not have the devotion to follow this career. My mother would come to visit me every Sunday. During one of her visits, I asked my mother if I could leave, she insisted that if I would just give it some time, I would adjust and learn to love it. She honestly felt it was the best place for me. Not to mention the sermons she would give me about how important and prestigious it was to have a priest in the family and how everyone would be so proud of me when I was ordained. Finally, after a year and a half, I was granted a three-month absence as I had expressed that my mother was having an operation and I needed time to find myself. While I was home, I realized that the seminary was not for me and that I did not want to become a priest.

Today when I read in the news about the abuse committed by priests, I find it hard to believe it's all true. I never saw or experienced any kind of abuse or molestation while attending the seminary. We lived there amongst other boys and multiple priests. We were always being told that if we saw or experienced any type of forbidden behavior on the part of students or priests that we were to report it immediately.

Back at home in Palma Soriano, I became friends with Alberto Sanchez whom everyone called Betico. Our mothers were friends and we were the exact same age. Betico's mother, Estrella, was very beautiful and won many beauty contests. Betico and I had many things in common. We both loved dolls and would go to the stores and admire the dolls. We also loved to go to the movies. Palma Soriano had three theatres, the Lupita Theatre, the Heredia Theatre, and the Encanto Theatre. The Lupita Theatre played only American films. The Heredia Theatre featured Spanish and Mexican films. This is where I saw every film of my favorite actor Maria Felix. The Heredia also hosted traveling live theatre shows. It was there that I first heard of a stripper getting arrested. Her name was Naja Karamuru. Many years later in New York I met and worked with her in the burlesque theatres and I reminded her of her arrest and we both had a great laugh. Lastly there was also the Encanto Theatre where they featured Italian, French and American western films. The Encanto was old and falling apart but the movies only cost ten cents. On the roof of the Encanto, there was a ravens' nest; they would sometimes fly and interrupt the films. People were used to it and didn't really pay attention after a while. Betico and I used to go to all the theatres depending upon what was showing. It was in the Lupita Theatre that we saw "Gone with the Wind" and where I fell in love with Clark Gable.

During these years my life would change forever. The Castro revolution was getting stronger and many of the schools had to close due to the fighting. Molotov Cocktails would be tossed through windows. The country was in chaos. Castro and his rebels were growing in strength. This is when my sister Irene and Idelphonso left Cuba for New York. 23

With the situation in Cuba, Mr. Smith closed his refineries. My father decided to retire and subsequently was diagnosed with lung cancer. Due to his condition my parents moved to Havana where he could receive better medical care. It was then that my father sat down to have a talk with me. He told me that he wanted me to leave Cuba. He called my godparents in New York and asked if they would allow me to live with them. They immediately said yes, so my father took me to the American Embassy to request a visa for permanent residency in the United States. They explained what was required for that type of visa. We supplied all the required paperwork and medical clearances; Irene was able to request for me as well. This was followed by my interview with the American Consul. He gave me my permanent resident visa to go to the United States, but I had to leave Cuba within three months, or my paperwork would be void.

Chapter 3 - Nefertiti, Baby and Bruno

Ralf Ferrer aka Nefertiti, and I became very good friends. When I told him that I wanted to live as a woman he said he would introduce me to his professional friends. These were queens who made their living as female impersonators. The first one I met was Baby Martel. He was beautiful as a boy or as a girl and was enormously talented. Baby invited me to his home in the east village for dinner with his lover Bobby. They were planning a trip for Baby to go to Paris. He had been contracted to play the Carrousel de Paris which was the most famous female impersonator club in Europe. Baby's friend Bruno Le Fantastique had arranged the contract for him. I told Baby that I had never seen a female impersonator show. He and Bobby invited me to the world-famous Apollo Theatre to see the Jewel Box Revue. The Jewel Box Revue was a troupe of twenty-five boys and one girl and were known as the best troupe of female impersonators.

When the curtains opened, I was instantly mesmerized by what I saw. It was as if I had entered a dream world. The costumes were so glamorous. The hats were enormous, there were feathers, sequins, and rhinestones to blind the audience all while singers crooned to the Great American Songbook and dancers paraded to the music. The emcee was Storme De Laverie, the only woman in the show and the very first king. As the show continued, I saw Bruno perform his famous half and half act. When Billie Day came to the stage as Billie Holiday singing in his own voice the songs that made her famous, it was impossible to tell that it wasn't her. He had studied her mannerisms and expressions and completely captured the essence of Billie Holiday. When the act was over, the standing ovation was thunderous. There was an assortment of other acts. At one point, Stormy pointed out that Josephine Baker was in the audience. Everyone stood to applaud her as she bowed. When the show was over, Baby took me back to the dressing rooms to meet everyone. As I was talking with Bruno, Josephine entered the room. This was the first time I met Josephine Baker. Josephine and Bruno knew each other from the Follies Bergere in Paris where they had performed together.

My relationship with Hector cooled off. He unfortunately wanted me to remain, although effeminate, still a boy. He wanted me to go to school and learn a trade such as beautician and to learn English to better myself. He most definitely did not want to see me in women's clothing. I told him that the reason I came to the United States was to become a woman. He was very upset about this and thus ended our relationship.

Bruno invited me to his birthday party celebration which was to be held at Ivan Hale's home. Ivan was an American poet and an art collector. Ivan's home was like a small castle. It was decorated with antiques and detailed in a French style with angels, cupids, and fine porcelains. The night of the party we were eight people sitting down for dinner. At the dinner table I was introduced to Armando and he spent the evening catering to me. After dinner he sat down at the baby grand piano and began playing, Gershwin. He dedicated to me, "That Man I Love". It was no secret that Armando had fallen in love with me. I liked him very much and he gave me his phone number to call him.

Chapter 4 – Armando Mendez

A few days after the party, I called Armando. He invited me to have dinner with him in Chinatown the following Saturday. I met Armando at his home which I describe as an antique shop with lots of paintings and a small library which was filled with all types of books in several languages including French, Spanish and others. He also owned a piano and violin. We had a cocktail and then headed to his favorite restaurant, Nom Wah Tea Parlor, which is still open in Chinatown.

At dinner he explained that he worked as a professor of literature, and he was a writer and a musician. He completely fascinated me with his culture and manners. Although he was eighteen years older than me, we began a love affair. I really liked Armando and he was very much "in love" with me. He was very knowledgeable about almost every culture on the planet and spoke the most beautiful Spanish. He told me once that he wanted to cultivate me. It was with Armando that I saw my first play, heard my first opera at the Met, and was able to meet my favorite actor since I was a child, Maria Felix. I was very happy at the time and I let Armando love me. He was a real friend to me especially when I received the news that my father had passed away. My godmother and godfather were also very fond of him.

Maria Felix came to New York in 1964 to the Puerto Rico Theatre in the Bronx, singing the songs of her husband, Agustin Lara. Armando had known her since he had been an entertainment critic columnist for newspapers and magazines in Mexico. Armando took me to see her show and after he sent a note backstage asking if Maria would see us. This was when I met Maria and I still have the photograph that she gave me that night.

Armando taught me literature and guided me in what was important to read. He introduced me to writers like Honore De Balzac, Oscar Wilde, Dante, and the American poet, Walt Whitman. My relationship with Armando was very pleasant and we were always busy with invitations and social engagements. I also spent time with my female impersonator friends.

I heard that there was going to be a Valentine's Day Ball at the Carter Hotel. I asked my godmother if she would make me a gown. The gown was brocade in metallic gold and silver. I bought rhinestone earrings, silver gloves, shoes and a silver purse. I went to Lubewsky in Harlem and had a custom shoulder length black wig made of human hair.

Armando escorted me to the ball. We had made reservations to have a table, which we shared with Jackie Morell, Luigi, Nefertiti and others. Armando ordered bottles of champagne for the table. We danced for a little while and then there was a drum roll and the emcee announced that the competition was starting. The emcee said that anyone who was interested in competing was to come to the left side of the stage to pick a number. Everyone at the table told me that I needed to go get a number and compete. I was number fifteen. We lined up and entered the stage. The band was playing a waltz while we paraded around showing our numbers to the judges. After the first pass, they called out ten numbers who would continue in the competition and I was among them. We did another walk and the emcee declared the winner to be number fifteen. I was so very happy that my mascara was running down my face because I never expected to win. I received a bouquet of flowers and an envelope with a hundred-dollar bill and was declared "The most beautiful drag queen in New York City". As I came out from the stage a man approached me with his business card. The card read, "Martinelli Attractions, Chi Chi LaVerne". He told me that he was the star of the Powderpuff Revue and would love for me to join them. I asked him what I would be doing, and he said that I would just be a showgirl and that they would train me.

I was beginning to have problems at home. I decided it would be best for my family and myself if I rented my own furnished room so that I could live my life as I pleased. I moved to a building on 76th and West End Ave., where many entertainers lived. This is where I met Lydia and Jimmy Del Rio. They were very popular adagio dancers in the New York cabarets. I became very good friends with Lydia. I died my hair blonde and would go out to the cabarets where she and Jimmy were working. One day, Lydia and I walked out of our building and the superintendent, who disliked me, called the police to report that there were two blondes walking on West End Ave. and that one of them was a man in drag. When the police came, they pulled Lydia's hair as if she was in drag. She went crazy showing her ID and talking about her children. After many apologies the police drove away never giving me a second look. This became a well-known story within the community.

I became friends with a group of people who would remain life-long friends. The only ones left are Sylvia Rivera, Susie Cardee, and Rafael Samalea. Out of all my non showbusiness group of friends we are the only four left after 55 years of friendship.

Having my own place allowed me the freedom to begin to collect different female articles of clothing and to allow my hair to grow. I could go out in drag whenever I wanted and didn't have to wait for the weekends. While Baby was working in Paris, Bruno and I struck up a good friendship. He even recommended me to Danny Brown, the owner of the Jewel Box Revue, for me to join the group as a showgirl.

A few months had passed when Baby returned from Paris. Our friendship grew even stronger than it had been. It was then that I felt comfortable to tell him that I wanted to be a woman. He brought me photos of the first French sex change, Coccinelle. Baby told me that he would talk to a pharmacist friend of his to see if I could get hormones. He put the first hormone pill on my tongue. He said, "What you want requires money and doctors. You should work as a female impersonator because you will lose your job at the factory."

Once I began the hormone treatment, the pharmacist recommended that I see Dr. Stern. I made an appointment and he began to give me weekly hormone injections at $10 each. He also recommended a psychiatrist for evaluation. It was required to have documentation from a psychiatrist at the time of the operation. I took his advice and began to see a psychiatrist. He never prescribed any medication, he only talked with me and asked me the following question. "Have you ever had sex with a woman?" I said that I had not and that I had never been attracted to women. There were many questions about my childhood including the first time I was attracted to a male.

At this time, Armando suggested that I give up my furnished room and move into his apartment. He was fine with me working as a female impersonator, but he did not want me to have anything to do with taking hormones and wouldn't allow me to discuss the possibility of a sex change. Obviously, I did not tell him that I was already taking female hormones or that I was seeing Dr. Stern.

New York was host to the 1964 World's Fair in Flushing Meadows in Queens. Armando and I visited the fair with some of our friends. We were mesmerized when we visited the Vatican Pavilion and saw Michelangelo's La Pieta. We also visited the Spanish Pavilion where we ate paella and watched the flamenco dancers into the evening.

On Sundays I would go to my godparents to have dinner. They were now living in Jamaica, New York. They had bought their dream home. On one of these visits, my sister called me to her bedroom for a private conversation. She was questioning me about what I was doing. She had noticed that my breasts had begun to grow. I showed her and explained that I was taking hormones. She hugged me and then gave me two pleated skirts from her closet. I knew from that moment on that I would have her support. I was also accepted and supported by my godfather and nephew no matter how I looked whenever I would visit.

My mother was now coming to live in the United States. She still had her Spanish passport, so she was able to leave Cuba. My sister, Irene had told my mother to expect the changes that she would see in me. I was so very happy that my mother would now be living near me. My sister, Mercedes, and her children went to live in Madrid. My sister, Micaela, and her husband and children came to the United States as well.

I decided not to move in with Armando and to keep my room. I was afraid of his reaction if I told him about seeing Dr. Stern and planning my future sex change. After a few months our love affair ended, but Armando and I continued to have a close friendship until his death in 2003.

Poems by Armando Mendez Fuentes

The lights go dim
as men file in,
avoiding each other's glances.
They sit
and they stare
into smoky, stale air
and wait
for
Marinka
Queen of the Runways.

The music starts,
the curtains part
and suddenly
a goddess
struts before them.
She bumps,
then she grinds
and she wiggles
her beautiful behind
as she must
for, she is
Marinka
Queen of the Runways.

As she swings her
curving hips
and wickedly licks
her red lips
the audience,
that many eyed beasts
devour her.
She stops
and then She starts
her wanton smile
gently breaking all our hearts
for we want her,
but we cannot have her
Fair Marinka
Queen of the Runways.

Her smile, so teasing.
Her body, so pleasing.
But her eyes
are filled with a
onesome sadness.
As her fiery gyrations
sear our imaginations,
she becomes a
different woman
for each of us.
Beautiful Marinka
Queen of the Runways.

In unshaven boys,
she sets their blood a boil
for she is all
warm and curving
woman.
And old, tired men
become young again
remembering
lush, lusty springs
and ripe, full
Septembers
thanks to
Marinka
Queen of the Runways.

Delicate as a lover's
whispered word.
Beauty rarer than
a tropical bird.
Her hair is the
color of midnight.
In her eyes
I have seen
Spanish castles,
gardenias, butterflies,
Kings and Queens.
She is the
Eve
I would forsake
Paradise for.
Lovely Marinka
Queen of the Runways.
Sweet Maria
Pearl of the Antilles

La Celebre Safo.

Este Poema esta dedicado a Melanie Hunter,
de mi Libro:El Canto Del Cisne.

Yo Adoro a Safo
De alma fogosa y cuerpo de palmera
De un rostro fino muy adorable.
La septimal muse., entre griegos fue
Sensual, cantora, erotica, poetisa cincelada
Entre columnas y plintos del cancel notable.

Su eterno talent conquisto bien la posteridad
Entre cisnes y alondras fue una majestad.,
Y una girnalda olorosa., por los festines.
A las sirvientas bellas de su mansion
dio., profundos besos de fuego y de passion
mientras las coronas con fragantes jazmines.

Al mar Jonico taciturna., partio un dia
Estando enferma, de amor y de poesia.
Extasiada quedo viendo la espuma del mar....
Vestia lino blanco, flores coronaban su cabeza,
Cuando recitaba sus versos a la naturaleza
Arrojandose al abismo se pudo asi matar.

Vi, el promotorio de Leucadia por el Jonico,
Con las sirenas goze un amor platonico,
Al recorder a Safo., senti una herida....
Golondrinas tristes volaban formando una constelacion,
Habia albos cisnes que filosofaron con meditacion
Por Safo, y el hondo misterio de la vida....

La mujer de Colatino se llamaba Lucrecia,
Se mato., como la musa de Grecia,
Safo por amor...la otra por virtuosa.
Se suicidaron algunos de Hegecias., el sofista,
! senor! porque se mata un artista?
? porque la Vida Humana es enganosa?

Chapter Five – The Powderpuff Revue

Johnny Martinelli and his brother Bernie were the owners of Martinelli Attractions. This was a theatrical agency that booked singers, comedians, and well-known exotic dancers. While Johnny owned two female impersonator revues, The Powderpuff and The Pandora Box, he also handled comedians and the burlesque features. His brother Bernie handled booking groups such as The Platters, Brooklyn Bridge, and The Chiffons to mention a few. He also represented Mae West in her night club act.

Chi Chi went with me to my meeting with Johnny Martinelli and I began rehearsals shortly after. They introduced me to Dorian Wayne to have him teach me the basics of being a showgirl before I was able to rehearse with the entire cast. Dorian was 5'10" with a medium build. He had dirty blonde hair with beautiful green eyes. He was very knowledgeable about how to be a showgirl and could be very demanding, however he was always sweet to me. The Powderpuff Revue worked locally Wednesday through Saturday or on the weekends only. We would go out on the road if the contract paid top dollar.

When I joined the cast, Chi Chi LaVerne was the star of the show, Karyl Houston was the singer, and Baby Martell was the exotic along with Dorian Wayne. Bobby Parissi was the belly dancer and Carlo was the comedian. The showgirls were Jamie Powers, and myself whom I called Sully. During the opening and finale production numbers all the acts would also perform as showgirls.

While I was working in the Powderpuff, Bobby Parissi was leaving the revue, so I started taking belly dance classes from Gulizar. She told me that I moved well and had a natural hand movement ability. She taught me how to play finger cymbals and to move around the stage. In my free time I would go to watch other belly dancers perform at the Grecian Palace and Istanbul Café. When Bobby left the group, I took his place in the lineup which then gave me a spot in the show. I was still doing the showgirl numbers for the opening and the finale. I was now making twenty more dollars per gig.

Working with the Powderpuff was a lot of fun. I got along well with Dorian and Baby, and Chi Chi just loved me. Mr. Martinelli had received good reports about me from Chi Chi and the club owners. He then decided to hire me to work club dates, as it was common to hire a female impersonator that could pass as a woman along with exotics. I was introduced as a belly dancer and after my performance I would pull my wig off and the emcee would say, "Mr. Sully, gentleman, Mr. Sully". The audience loved it as they all had believed I was a girl. The feature was the only act that could follow. I loved those gigs and I made good money.

Club dates were gigs that were stand alone events. They took place in hotels, restaurants, catering houses, social clubs or even a firehouse. They varied in purpose from corporate anniversaries, Christmas parties, retirement parties, fundraisers or stag parties. They could consist of a solo act or multiple acts. I also worked club dates for political campaigns. New York and Chicago were the capitals of the club dates and entertainers who did not want to travel could make a living just working them.

I was beginning to make a name for myself as a female impersonator and was being booked in other revues like The Pandora Box and the Boys Will Be Girls. Joey Tone from Pandora Box and Leslie Marlow from Boys Will Be Girls would offer me work when they knew the Powderpuff did not have a gig. Franky Quinn and Mr. Tish would also call me to work for shows. The agent who handled these other revues was Mr. Eddie Kaplan.

The female impersonator revues were all rivals of one another, and each club owner had their favorite. All the performers in the revue had to perform with a live band. The singers did not have to have a lot of natural feminism and were therefore easier to hire. However, the dancers, exotics, and belly dancers required a male who looked more feminine because their bodies would be exposed to the audience. Belly dancers were rare and very much in demand. Because of this I found work with multiple revues.

Mr. Martinelli booked the Pandora Box at the Living Room Nightclub in Boston. Joey Tone, the star and emcee of the Pandora Box, called to hire me as the belly dancer and was going to have the fabulous King August as his singer, Baby Martell as the exotic and the comedian was going to be Billy Camp.

We were initially booked for four weeks and ended up staying for two months. When I told Chi Chi I was going to work with the Pandora Box in Boston he was so upset that he complained to Mr. Martinelli that Joey Tone had taken me away from him. Johnny Martinelli had to call a meeting with the three of us. He said that we all had to work where the job is and that no one owned anyone and that they all needed to share the acts. Since Johnny owned both revues there was nothing Chi Chi could say about it. There was, however, something he could do. Chi Chi asked me to move into his apartment at 44th St and 8th Ave. He had a large apartment and felt that it would help me save more money.

I had a lot of fun living with Chi Chi. We would go out frequently and see Broadway shows. Marlene Dietrich came to Broadway for a ten-day concert stand. We got tickets to the show and through Chi Chi's contacts we were able to meet her. I still have the autographed photo she gave me that night.

Martinelli booked the Powderpuff at the Showboat in Nantucket, Massachusetts. The Showboat was an actual decommissioned ferry that had been turned into a nightclub. Chi Chi booked Karyl Houston, the comedian Billy Camp, Jamie Powers as an exotic and me as the belly dancer. We were supposed to perform the entire summer from Memorial to Labor Day. The show had been received very well but after four weeks Chi Chi told me that he was going to replace me. He explained that the owners of the nightclub felt that I looked too much like a woman for a female impersonator revue. Chi Chi replaced me with the exotic impersonator, Vicki Lynn, who became famous when she starred in Teaserama with Bettie Page. Chi Chi told me to call Johnny and he would find me other work in Boston. I called Johnny and he booked me into the The Other Side nightclub. I really enjoyed the nightclub, but I did not want to stay there. I was living as a female and this had become a source of ridicule from other impersonators. The Other Side boys did not welcome me and were extremely nasty. I did not want to work in that type of environment.

I went back to New York and worked weekends and club dates. My friend Toni Carroll got me a job with her ex-partner during the day. I went to work for designer Frank Page in his atelier. I learned the art of beading and working on costumes. I met many of his clients, but it was Della Reese who requested Frank to be her personal designer on her new talk show in Los Angeles. I had the good fortune to work with Frank for several months and before he left for Hollywood, he made me two very beautiful gowns. I would wear one of those Frank Page gowns in my feature burlesque debut.

In the sixties I would go to the Palladium as this was the place to be for Latin orchestras and dancing. The Palladium had two different ballrooms with two different orchestras at the same time. They had dancers who performed in front of the orchestra for the audience to follow the Latin rhythm. It was open nightly at eight in the evening and Sundays at one in the afternoon. My friend Graciela Romero was the foster sister of Machito. I was also good friends with Tito Puentes' girlfriend, Guille Averoff. All the famous Latin musicians played the Palladium. It was one of my favorite places to spend time with my show business friends.

Many artists were coming to America as refugees from Cuba. The Watusis were some of those artists. They were an Afro Cuban Trio and their lead dancer was

38

Gloria Ochoa. Gloria and I became very good friends. She introduced me to many people who I would also become friends with. I met Eduardo Davidson who wrote "La Pachanga" and the Cuban soprano Marta Peres, who was a famous opera singer with the New York Metropolitan Opera. I also met Jose Manuel Partagas (pepe la millonaria). With Pepe I always had a great time. He was from a very prestigious family in Cuba and worked for a Spanish Duchess in New York whose home on Park Avenue was like a small museum. It was with Pepe that I met Salvador Dali.

I had admired his art enormously, but when I met Salvador Dali, he seemed like a madman. He was very eccentric with a penetrating stare. I wasn't sure if he was looking at me with desire or that he just didn't know where to place me. Pepe told me later that Dali was interested in getting to know me better, but his reputation scared me. Maria Felix once said that Dali began his career pretending to be crazy and then actually became crazy.

Soon I received a contract to go to San Juan, Puerto Rico to work in El Cotorrito (The Little Parrot). Johnny Rodriguez was the owner of the El Cotorrito. He was the lead singer of a guitar trio that travelled all over the world. Along with myself, they also booked my friend Baby Martell. Once again Baby managed to find a pharmacist who would sell me hormones. While working there I became friends with Myrta Silva. She was working on her own television show in San Juan. I liked working there very much and I got to meet all the singers and actors who came to San Juan.

Dorian Wayne was my favorite of all the American female impersonators. He looked like Anita Ekberg when he was in drag. When he was out of drag, he was the most handsome man. Dorian was a natural beauty and always kind to me. I loved working with him. His charisma on stage was contagious. One day in the dressing room I asked him why he didn't get a sex change. He opened his big green eyes and said to me, "Honey if I did that and didn't marry a millionaire, I would have to keep working in these joints. I would end up killing myself."

The Powderpuff Revue was booked into Buffalo NY, for four weeks in the nightclub, McVan's. While performing at McVan's, the AGVA, American Guild of Variety Acts, came in and I had to join the union as it was a union club. The show was so successful that four weeks turned into four months. While working at McVan's, Christine Jorgensen had a ten-day engagement with the club but refused to work with female impersonators. She would only work with Chi Chi because he was a singer, comedian and the emcee. Therefore, the cast was sent to Niagara Falls to work in the Polynesian Club. When this happened, I had a major panic attack because my idol was coming to the club where I was working, and I had so many questions to ask her and was so excited to be able to work with her and she refused. Chi Chi told her about me and asked if I could meet with her one Sunday and she agreed. We had a conversation in the dressing room, and she gave me some very good advice and referred me to Dr. Harry Benjamin, who wrote the book, "The Transsexual Phenomenon". I promised her that when I was back in New York City I would go and see him. I went into the audience to watch her perform. She was exquisitely feminine and told small jokes between her songs. She wore five different gowns during one performance. Her show ended with a question and answer session and after the show she autographed copies of her biography. I cannot express what I felt at the time. How does one feel when they have just met their idol?

After the engagement in Buffalo ended, I traveled back to New York. I went to see Dr. Benjamin and he gave me a letter that said that I was in his care and asked the authorities to treat me with the same respect they would a biological woman. He also sent me to see another psychiatrist for a new evaluation.

The Powderpuff Revue always included one female exotic. While working at The Paddock Club, in Yonkers, New York, the female exotic was Cookie Nelson. Cookie and I became very good friends. We would drink every night with horse owners and jockeys from the racetrack that was just across the way from the Paddock. The audience refused to believe that I was a boy. Chi Chi and club staff were always insisting that I was. Cookie asked me, "Why don't you just work as a girl since everyone already thinks you are?" She told me that she knew an agent that she would refer me to for work as a girl. The agent she was speaking of was Bobby Colt. The following week, Leslie Marlow contacted me to work with his show, Boys Will Be Girls Revue, for a weekend at The Continental in White Plains, New York.

I really liked working there. They had a very affluent audience. It was there that I had my first taste of French champagne. I worked this show with Robin Rogers, Bunny Lake, Frankie Bennett and Dorian Wayne.

One evening while sitting at a table with a couple, the owner wagered them a bottle of champagne regarding my gender. I told them that I was a boy. This was a great surprise to them as most of the audiences believed that I was the one "girl" in the show. I told them about my transitioning which was a whole new idea to them. They found it to be quite intriguing. The owner won the wager since they already knew my gender, but we were treated to a bottle of Moet & Chandon Imperial Brut anyway.

That night, Leslie Marlow was so upset that he called me off to the side and told me that I would not be working with them anymore. He said he had a female impersonator revue and that I no longer fit the description. I responded that it was fine and that I had other work. I told him the only one I would miss was Dorian. This was not what he expected to hear.

I called Joey Tone who ran The Pandora Box Revue. I explained what happened with Leslie Marlow and he began to laugh. He told me he was going to call me anyway. He had a gig for me in Long Island. I went to work with The Pandora Box and the show was very successful. They kept us for four weeks at a club called The Infirmary, in Babylon, New York. I had the most fabulous time working with Joey. He treated me like his little sister, and we had fun running around town hanging out in all the clubs. This would be the last time I worked as a female impersonator.

SULLY

1965 Sully

1967 Marinka
46

47

1968 Marinka

Marinka

1968 Marinka

James J.
Kriegsmann
N.Y.

51

My agent Johnny Martinelli, Bruno le Fantastique,
Dorian Wayne and Baby Martell

1968 Powderpuff Revue
Kurt Mann, Sully, Chi Chi LaVerne, Karyl Houston and Jamie Powers

Nefertiti with his ocelot Delilah

Chapter 6 - Bobby Colt

Bobby Colt was an agent who had been married to Hope Diamond. He had been the production singer of the Copacabana Nightclub prior to becoming an agent. As I walked into the office with Cookie, I met his new wife, Cathy, who was also his receptionist. She greeted us with many warm pleasantries. We were called into Bobby's office and the first thing he told me was how beautiful he thought I was. He asked us to sit and thanked Cookie for bringing me to him. He began to ask me questions about who I worked for and what type of act I did. I answered and Cookie asked to speak with Bobby alone. I excused myself to wait in reception until he called for me. After a few minutes, Bobby called me back into his office. He told me he was aware of my situation and that he would book me if we kept my situation a secret. He took my photos and commented that I was prettier in person. He also told me that I needed a new name. He thought that I looked like Tina Louise, so he wanted to call me Tina Darling. He then asked Cathy to make three contracts for me for the Kent Rose Club in Middletown, Lorenzo's Supper Club in Schenectady, and Andre's in Syracuse. Bobby explained to me that he booked a dozen clubs all around New York state. He told me it would take me three months to tour all of them. He said he would always keep me working and reiterated that I absolutely had to keep the secret. He explained that he would get ten percent commission. This was very new to me as now I was becoming my own business. He told me to get new photos and asked if I had any questions. The only thing I had a bit of a problem with was the name Tina Darling. He said, "We will use the name for now." He opened a drawer full of photos of famous exotic dancers who he represented and told me that he would also make me a star.

Cookie and I left Bobby Colt's office and went across

the street to an Argentinian restaurant named Gauchos for dinner. At dinner we discussed her helping me with an exotic dancer routine as up to this point, I had only done showgirl and belly dancing. When we left the restaurant, Cookie took the subway and I walked to 71st St to my home. On the way, I had the thought, "How am I going to go down to a g-string?" I supposed I could wear two at the same time.

When I got home, I called a couple of exotic friends of mine. The first was Toni Carroll and she kept trying to tell me to work as a belly dancer. But belly dancers did not make much money per week and had to depend on tips. Princess Kahlua was offended. She said, "How dare you?!" She thought the idea was crazy. After multiple negative responses, I knew I needed to find an answer. So, I put on two g-strings, but it didn't work. That's when I thought to use tape. I went to the shower and shaved my genitals completely. After, I went to the corner pharmacy and asked for the widest, strongest tape there was. The tape they recommended was two and a half inches wide and the best adhesive tape on the market. I went home and with just a few pieces of tape I was able to tape my genitalia all the way to the back.   Once I figured out the taping, one g-string was enough, but you could still see the wide white tape. The next day I went to Woolworth's to see if there was something I could use to cover the tape. I came across hair nets. I went home and with spirit gum I glued the hair net on to the tape which gave the effect of a "hairy pussy". The only problem I had was that I had to do that taping at home and could not use the restroom until I returned. This was very difficult and caused me much stress, but I did it anyway.

My boyfriend at the time was Doug Hunter. That weekend we went to his parents' house for his mother's birthday party. When I met his grandmother, she was introduced to me as Marinka. The name fascinated me. The following Monday I went to see Bobby and told him I did not want anything to do with the Tina Darling business. I was uncomfortable with the name. I told him that I had a new name, and that was Marinka. He said he wanted me to use a name with more star quality. I said "I like the name Marinka. I think it's very beautiful for a dancer." Bobby called for Cathy and asked her to change my name in the contracts to Marinka.

That week I met with Cookie for her to assist me with my routines. We decided I would do a belly dance strip at the first and third show and I would use a gown and panels during the second show. In one week, I put my acts together and went to the Music World and bought sheet music of every tune I would be using. The following Wednesday I took the greyhound bus to Middletown. I went to the Kent Rose where they gave me the room near the owner's; they housed the exotic upstairs in the owner's apartment. I had a private room but shared the bathroom with Kent and Rose. The first thing Kent told me was that they had a rule that no client can ever come upstairs under any circumstance. I opened at the Kent Rose to enormous success. The schedule was Wednesday through Sunday. On Monday I went home and visited Bobby to pay his commission. He told me that if everyone liked me as much as Kent Rose, I wouldn't have any problems getting work.

The next day I took the greyhound bus to Schenectady. When I arrived at Lorenzo's I found that it was a much bigger club than the Kent Rose had been. I opened at Lorenzo's and if he liked my act, he was supposed to keep me for two weeks. By that Thursday when I hadn't heard anything from Lorenzo regarding the option for the second week, I called Bobby and told him to go ahead and book me somewhere else. On Saturday, after my last show, I went to pick up my pay from the office. Lorenzo told me that I was a good act, but I needed a "bust job". I had never heard that expression before and I thought it was very rude of him. I took my pay and left. That evening in my hotel I had a nightmare, imagining myself with two big ugly cantaloupes on my chest. The only breast implants I had seen were very unattractive.

On Monday I went to Bobby to pay my commission

from Lorenzo's. He already knew what Lorenzo had told me. Bobby told me that Lorenzo thought I was a good act. It was too late for Bobby to book me in another club, so I had to wait until the following week to work at my booking in Syracuse. Bobby also told me that he knew of a doctor in Yonkers by the name of Dr. Benito Rish that was doing marvelous work with silicone.

Going to Dr. Benito Rish's office was like entering the circus. There were women from every walk of life. Procedures were made on demand, silicone injections, nose jobs, and every other procedure that a plastic surgeon can do. This also included sex change operations. Sitting in the waiting room, I met Park Avenue madams, exotic dancers, call girls, and other characters. The office staff was a bunch of gossiping ladies. Once you got to know them, they would tell you what everyone else was visiting the office for. I knew that when I turned around, they would be talking about me as well. A madam that I talked to asked me what I did for a living. I told her I was an exotic dancer. She offered me a job in her house on Park Avenue where the girls made a minimum of a thousand dollars a week, making her clients happy and making their wishes and fantasies come true. I thanked her but turned her down for obvious reasons.

When my name was called to finally see Dr. Rish, he asked what I wanted to do, and I told him that I wanted silicone injections as I was an exotic dancer. He suggested implants and I told him that my friends had them done and I didn't like them. He then proceeded to tell me that he was the one who had done their surgeries as he recognized their names. Dr. Rish then said that with three sets of double treatments I would get a considerable volume to my breasts. I would receive these treatments for three consecutive weeks. After that we would look to see the volume and decide then if I would want to go larger. I decided to have my first treatment that day. After the three treatments my breasts were a full 36 C.

At home I had to alter my bra because my breasts were larger, and I had a full cleavage. When I opened

58

in Syracuse, I noticed that the audience received me even more now that I had my new breasts. I continued traveling to Rochester, Utica, and Lake George making three hundred fifty dollars a week. This was when I first felt like a part of show business. Bobby Colt was very happy with me and I had become one of his top exotics. I opened many doors for Bobby.

In the meantime, I was saving money for my sex change operation. I was on the road traveling through New York and Pennsylvania for four to six weeks before taking a week off, then I would do the entire circuit again. This was when I would meet the love of my life.

Chapter 7 – Meeting Rod

I had just left a friend's house and was walking along 8th avenue when I heard a car pull up next to me and a man asked "Lady. Did you call a taxi?" I replied, "No." The man said, "Can a taxi call you?" I looked inside the taxi and saw this gorgeous man behind the wheel. We chatted for a few minutes and he offered to drive me home off the meter. I got into the taxi and he introduced himself as Rod. I told him my name was Marinka. He asked me where I lived, and I told him I lived on 71st between Columbus and Central Park. We had a conversation on the way home. He asked me what I did for a living. I told him I was an exotic dancer and he jumped in his seat and was so excited as he had never met an exotic before. He went on to ask me where I worked. I told him that I would be performing next in Middletown at the Kent Rose. He screamed and said, "I will be near there in Monticello!" He explained that he had a horse that he liked to play there and would be spending the weekend. By this time, we were at 71st and Broadway in front of a coffee shop named Ham and Eggs. He asked me if I would like to get a drink. We went into the coffee shop and when the waitress came to the table she said, "Hello Sully." Rod said, "I thought your name was Marinka?" I explained to him that before I became an exotic dancer, my name was Sully. We talked about many things and the more we talked the more I liked him. He had a fantastic personality. I had an iced tea and Rod had coffee. When we finished our drinks, he walked me the rest of the way home. I gave him my phone number and told him that I would see him in Middletown that weekend.

The very next day my phone rang. It was Rod inviting me to Nathan's in Coney Island to try the lobster rolls. I accepted and he picked me up in his private car. We drove all the way to Coney Island, had some lobster rolls and sat in the sand watching the ocean. When he kissed me, I knew I was falling in love with him.

On Wednesday, I took my usual greyhound bus to Middletown. When I performed at the Kent Rose, it was only me and a two-piece band. I always had a lot of fun working there and meeting new people. The Kent Rose had a great selection of music on the jukebox and I would play it when the band was on break. I would dance around the room from table to table to the bar. Everyone loved me and I was like the Queen of the Kent Rose, especially because I was the only girl there. Even with the usual fun being had, all I was thinking about was when Rod was going to come.

On Saturday night, for the first show I didn't see Rod and was down, thinking I was just a taxi ride. When I came out for the second show, Rod was sitting in the first seat at the bar. He knew I wouldn't be able to miss him sitting there. I saw his big black eyes staring at me. When I finished the show, I went over to him and he told me that I had a beautiful body and danced beautifully. We spent the evening having a couple of drinks. He asked me out on a date for the next day. I agreed but I had to be back to the Kent Rose by 7pm. He said he would take me to brunch. I told him to meet me in front of the club.

That morning I wore a summer dress with a big floppy hat. We had breakfast and then headed out to Monticello. I had never been to the Monticello racetrack, so he took me there and showed me around. We went to the Concord Hotel for cocktails and then out to dinner. This was the most beautiful day I had ever had with a man. At the end of the day I knew I was in love with him.

Our friendship continued and Rod wanted to have physical relations with me. I tried to tell him about my situation a few times, but Rod would interrupt me and tell me that he didn't want to know my past. I told my friend, Gladys, about the situation with Rod. She suggested that her boyfriend, Frank, could maybe talk to him if we went out for a double date.

We went to dinner and Rod and Frank got along well. Frank suggested that we go to the Inner Circle club for music and drinks. We had to take seats at the bar as there were no tables available. One of the bartenders recognized me and told Frank that his tall friend was not a girl, but that they were a boy. Rod overheard this. When Frank tried to put the bartender off and said that he was mistaken, the bartender insisted that he knew me as Sully from the Silhouette in Brooklyn where he also bartended. The bartender said, "Hello Sully. Remember me?" I said, "Yes." Rod heard all of this. After a couple of drinks, we left the club and drove Gladys and Frank to their homes. I was now alone in the car with Rod. Rod told me that he needed to know if it was true. I said, "I tried twice to tell you, but you didn't want to hear about my past." He said, "I could not have ever imagined this. This will change everything." In this moment, I couldn't talk. I was so ashamed that Rod had to find out this way. I was overwhelmed with emotion. My heart was breaking, and I couldn't think. Rod was the first man who I had built a real relationship with. It was based on respect and trust and was much more than an affair. I felt like the sky and the earth were closing in on me. I wanted to say so many things to him. I wanted to tell him that I was ashamed and that I was not laughing at him, but nothing would come out. He turned on the radio and turned up the volume and drove me home. When we got to my place, I got out of the car and managed to tell him that I was so very sorry. I shut the car door and Rod drove away.

I left New York to open at the Silver Slipper in Washington DC the following Monday. Bobby Colt had explained to me that this was a light mixing club. I had never worked a mixing club before, but Bobby said, "If Sam likes you, he can keep you there indefinitely." That evening while sitting at the bar, Sam gave a speech to all the dancers. The rules of the house were that we could not leave the club with a client. Everyone had to wear long skirts. We couldn't wear pants or short skirts in the club, and we must sit at the table in the back of the club and wait for the maître d' to bring us to the clients. We were not allowed to be at the bar either. The only ones 63 who could work the bar were, Zi Zi Martini and Carmela, the Sophia Loren of burlesque, as they had worked there for a long time and had the trust of the owners. We weren't to give out phone numbers or accept tips from the clients. When a client asked what we were drinking, we were to say, "champagne". Dancers were only to drink champagne with the clients. Not long after this speech the maître d' asked me to come with him to a table where two gentlemen were waiting. I sat down at the table and the maître d' brought a bottle of champagne. Shortly after, I received my 20-minute call to perform my act and therefore had to excuse myself from the gentlemen's company. We were only allowed twenty minutes to get dressed. If we ran behind the emcee would make a joke; "Well ladies and gentlemen, I think Marinka is having trouble finding her g-string." He would continue covering until I was ready. When I was finished with my show, I expected to return to the gentleman's table, but I was informed that my presence had been requested at another. That was how easy mixing was at the Silver Slipper. A couple of days later Sam told me that I would be staying there for the next three weeks until I would have to leave for Baltimore to fulfill my contracts at the Les Girls and The Two O'Clock.

The Silver Slipper was like no other club that I could have ever dreamed of working for. I was constantly mesmerized by the caliber of the clients. One night you could be sitting with Wilbur Mills, the representative from Arkansas and the most powerful man in Washington and the next night with Ted Kennedy. Ted Kennedy asked me the first time I sat with him, why the Cubans don't like the Kennedy Family. I told him because of what happened with the "Bay of Pigs". You may have also found yourself sitting with J. Edgar Hoover. Hoover, the first director of the FBI, never seemed like he was there for recreation but more to keep an eye on what everyone else was doing. He usually would be sitting with Bill Crespo, the male adagio dancer at the Slipper. I didn't know who some of these people were when I sat down with them and my

English was limited so there wasn't much I could say to them. I only knew they were important men because the staff at the club told me so. At the end of the week I had two payments coming to me. I had an envelope with two hundred fifty dollars which was my salary for the week and an even bigger envelope with four hundred dollars which was my commission for the week. I didn't ever want to leave the Slipper. My last week there Sam gave me the option to be a house girl. I told him that I would have to discuss it with Bobby once I was finished with my contracts.

I went back to New York for two days before heading to Baltimore. My phone rang and it was Rod. He wanted to know where I had been. I told him that I had been in Washington and that the owner of the club extended my contract and then offered me a steady position. Rod was very jealous and told me that he didn't want me to work there. This was the first time he had ever said something to me regarding my work. That's when I knew he still cared. I apologized to him again. I told him that I had a lot I wanted to tell him. We decided to have dinner the following night at the Hawaii Kay. This was the Polynesian restaurant that would become our place to go every Sunday for years to come. We always had an appetizer sampler followed by our favorite dish, Cornish hen stuffed with fried rice, along with a mai tai cocktail while watching the Polynesian show.

Rod offered me his support and friendship. He wanted to know when I would be having my sex change operation. I told him that I had been doing all this extra work to save the money I needed for the procedure and now that I had the money, I needed to find a surgeon. I explained to Rod that I had interviewed with the doctors at Johns Hopkins Hospital when I was in Washington, and that they informed me that they had a five-year waiting list. I also explained about the Benito Rish circus of surgery that was available in Yonkers and that I had no intention of letting him touch me. And the other option was in Casablanca, Morocco. I told Rod that I was always asking my doctors if they had heard of any other options but at that time there wasn't. This was the 1960's and this type of surgery was rare and not easy to come by. Very few doctors were interested in doing these procedures for one reason or another. All I could do was follow the guidelines of Dr. Benjamin.

Chapter 8 - Mixing Clubs

Bobby sent me to Baltimore to work at the Les Girls Cabaret. This club was a bit outside of the famous "Baltimore Block". It was a mixing club with an old-time atmosphere. The club preferred older women, so I was the youngest girl there. The feature that week was a statuesque beauty by the name of Libby Jones. Libby was a 5'11" blond with large breasts and a beautiful body. She was a great performer and always a joy to watch. She was featured on an album cover and wrote a book that gave instructions on how to do striptease. Libby was a featured performer in the 1950's and 60's. She would often ask me why I didn't work in the burlesque theatres. I explained that I preferred the clubs and that I had only worked with Bobby and the Martinelli's who had always kept me busy. She told me she would speak to Sam Cohen about me. Sam owned the Follies Burlesque on 44th and Broadway in New York City.

My next booking was in Blaze Starr's famous Two O'Clock which was located in the "block" in Baltimore. After I finished my first show, I went to a table in the back as I was accustomed to doing at the Silver Slipper and at Les Girls. I was waiting to be requested. No one offered me a drink or requested me, so I just sat at the table alone all night. When I returned the following evening, Blaze asked me why I just sat at the table alone. I explained that I was waiting to be requested. She said, "Here in the Two O'Clock we do things differently." I explained to her that I was not accustomed to going to a table or up to the bar and asking a man for a drink. I didn't know how to do that. Blaze told me that I can either sit there all night and only receive my performance salary, or I can talk to and be friendly with the customers and make a large commission. She then said, "Come with me." She took me to a table, introduced me and then left me there with the men who had greeted me so graciously. After that the bottles of champagne flowed!

Blaze also introduced me to her partner and agent Sal Goodman. Sal told me that if I wanted to be someone in this business, I needed a manager. I asked him how much he charged, and he told me a minimum of twenty percent. I knew I wasn't interested, especially at that rate, but I told him I would consider it.

At the Two O'Clock, I would place myself strategically at the bar before and in between my shows. I found out that I couldn't talk to just anyone. The barmaid told me that when a man sat at the bar, I could respond with a "hello" but that I wasn't to get into a conversation with a stranger until she had screened him. She also told me that if she placed a little white bar towel in front of the customer in the tip tray, he had not been screened. She would ask where he was from, check the label of his tie, ask him why he was in Baltimore and how long he was staying, etc. Once she went through her usual song and dance of questions, she would remove the towel and then I could talk with that customer, but only if they started the conversation. These conversations usually began with the customer asking if they could buy me a drink. After having the first drink at the bar, you could then move to a table to have a more private conversation. The waiters knew the regulars and would tell us that it was okay to engage them in conversation.

Blaze was very good to me and taught me the art of mixing. It really was an art and it required more than just a pretty face. People came to the Two O'Clock just to meet Blaze. She would greet them and initially sit with them. When they offered champagne, she would toast with them and then she would call one of her favorites to the table and give them the opportunity to have that client as she would excuse herself. Many of these clients would enjoy the conversation and would fall in love with you. They were trying to get to know you better on a personal level to try and date you outside of the club.

Mixing clubs have always had a stigma attached to them. Dancers who had never worked in a mixing club

68

were apprehensive about it. There were often assumptions made about what would happen with the men in those clubs. I hear a lot of women who I worked with denying that they worked in mixing clubs.

My experience with mixing clubs was very favorable. The mixing clubs always had a better stage and a better band than a supper club. We had the protection of the bouncers and in some cases, we even had the protection of the police as most of the mixing clubs were owned by La Cosa Nostra.

Supper clubs only hired dancers who worked as a feature. The reason for this was there was only one dancer in the show, therefore she had to be good with a great act and a great wardrobe that could carry the show.

There were burlesque clubs that hired multiple dancers and an emcee. These clubs hired mostly females and local acts. The feature would work one week only, and the house girls received a limited salary since the work was steady. There were very few of this type of club.

In the mixing clubs the feature had the option of whether they wanted to mix or not. It was not expected of them, but if she did, she was compensated well through commission on alcohol sales. Most features, however had "no mixing" written into their contract.

Mixing clubs had rules that the dancers were required to follow. The first rule was that you could not allow a customer to touch you. Dresses were required. Pants were not allowed. You could not give out any personal information including your phone number. The biggest of them all was that you could not leave the club with a client. If a bouncer saw you, you would be immediately terminated.

Most of the successful mixers were the "big girls". They were called this because they could sell multiple bottles of champagne a night and usually worked steadily in the clubs for months or years on end. These women were good at "using the glass". The glass was a twenty-ounce plastic cup filled halfway with ice. The girls would pretend to drink water from the cup but were actually spitting out the champagne. Because these girls were good for increasing alcohol sales, they would often stay in one club as a "house girl".

"The Block" in Baltimore was a city block full of strip clubs and the best one was the Two O'Clock. Another notorious club on the block was the Inferno. Like some of the other clubs, the Inferno had "separates". A separate was a table or booth enclosed by curtains where the client could spend private time with the dancer. When the client ordered a bottle of champagne the waiter would close the curtains and not return until twenty minutes later. Some of the dancers could keep a man in the separate all evening. I cannot speak to what transpired as I never went into a separate. The most successful "separate girl" was a woman who had a wooden leg. She was very famous throughout the block.

There were different types of mixing clubs. There were the first-class clubs where you mixed by request with elegance and friendliness. The second-class mixing clubs were "clip joints". I never worked in this type of club.

The Best of The Mixing Clubs:

Silver Slipper, Washington DC
The Gold Rush, Washington DC
Blaze Starr's Two O'clock, Baltimore MD
Les Girls in Baltimore
The Teddy bear in Boston
The Two O'clock in Boston
Alphonso's (Big Al, Riviera Beach, MA
The Purple Onion, Greenwich Village, NY
The Cinderella Club, Greenwich Village, NY
The Candy Bar, West Palm Beach, FL
Place Pigalle, Miami Beach, FL
Sex Stop, Chicago, IL
Sho Bar, New Orleans, LA
Carousel, Dallas, TX

Some of these clubs were operated by La Cosa Nostra, or organized crime. Mixing clubs eventually morphed into what is known today as a strip club with one big difference, we were not allowed to be touched by a client. Where else in the world would a girl like me have met and drank champagne with a senator, politician, or millionaire, if not in a mixing club. Many girls found husbands or lifetime friends who would always look out for them like Blaze Starr's relationship with the Louisiana Governor and Fanny Fox with Wilbur Mills. Most of the mixing clubs were closed after the media exposed the "Stripper and the Congressman" scandal of the Basin in 1975. Mixing clubs gave girls the opportunity to meet people who they otherwise never would.

Chapter Nine – Dr. Prado

I returned to New York when my contract with the Two O'Clock was up. For a while I had been looking for a surgeon for my operation. One afternoon I walked into Victor's Café on 71st and Columbus Avenue and ran into my old friend, Myrta Silva. She called me over to her table and asked me if I was "complete". I told her that I hadn't found the right doctor, so she offered me the phone number of a friend of hers, Dr. Frank Prado.

I called Dr. Prado's office to arrange a consultation. I called to tell Rod that I had a consultation scheduled with a doctor the next day at 2 p.m. and he said that he would go with me. I went to the bank and removed eight hundred dollars to use as a down payment if the doctor would give me a date for the surgery and I felt comfortable with him. I called a friend who I knew had some plastic surgery performed by Dr. Prado. She highly recommended him.

When I arrived for my appointment, I gave my name Sully to the receptionist. She mentioned that Myrta had called to let them know that I was her friend. She gave me forms to complete and when I returned the forms to her, she could not believe her eyes. She saw my legal name and what procedure I was there for on the form and she just couldn't believe that I was a boy. I waited to be called in to see the doctor and eventually I went in alone while Rod waited for me in reception. The doctor and I chatted for a few minutes regarding our mutual friend, Myrta Silva. He asked me how long I had been taking hormones and if I had been for a psychological evaluation. He wanted to know which doctors were treating me since he would need letters from them for me to enter the hospital for surgery. I gave him the letter that I had brought with me from Dr. Harry Benjamin. Dr. Prado explained that I needed to be completely naked and asked his assistant to bring me a robe. After I was undressed, he examined me and asked if he could take photos. He was bothered by the fact that I had silicone injected into my breasts.

Dr. Prado explained that there were two steps to this operation. The first step was a very simple procedure that he would do there in the office. This was the castration and the charge was five hundred dollars. He then explained that I would return in one week to have the stitches removed. The second part of the surgery would take place after waiting two or more months to be sure everything was healed, and after he had the letters from Dr. Stern, Dr. Benjamin and from the psychiatrist.

The second part of the surgery was to be performed at the Seven Arts Hospital. For that part of the surgery his fee would be three thousand dollars, paid up front one week prior to the procedure. The hospital fee would be fifteen hundred dollars and another five hundred dollars for the anesthesiologist paid in full when I checked into the hospital. I told Dr. Prado that I had the money in my purse and that I could do the first part of the procedure that day. He asked his nurse to get Dr. Benjamin on the phone. He returned to the room and told me he would do the procedure right then.

Dr. Prado gave me a few injections in the pubic region to numb the area. He was surprised to see that the nurse wouldn't have to shave me. My skin was irritated and red from the tape. When I told him what I had been doing in order to perform, he started to laugh. He then made an incision about an inch long and removed my testicles. Dr. Prado held them up for me to see. This was one of the happiest moments of my life and I was happy to know they were gone. The incision only required a few stitches and had to remain clean by applying gauze with saline solution twice a day to the area. He told me that I would experience some bleeding for the next few days. I was not allowed to do anything active as to cause more bleeding. I was to go home and relax. I went out to reception, made my appointment to remove the stitches in one week and left for home with Rod.

When I went to see Dr. Benjamin to get my letters for the surgery, he told me that I was lucky; Dr. Prado didn't want to do any more sex change operations. I told him that a good friend of his referred me, so he accepted me as a patient.

I called Bobby Colt and told him that I needed two weeks off. I explained that I had found a doctor in New York and that I had already had the first part of the operation performed. I needed to rest and then go see my other doctors to get the release letters from them. This, in and of itself, was a whole process as I would make an appointment and then they would prepare the letters for me to pick up at my next appointment. Bobby was surprised to hear of my procedure and was completely understanding. He had no problem giving me two weeks to rest and get my affairs in order, but Bobby did let me know that I was booked in two weeks at one of the best strip clubs in New York, The Purple Onion.

Chapter 10 – The Follies Burlesk

Bobby called to ask me to go to the Follies Burlesk with him. He said that Sam Cohen had called and wanted to meet me. I accepted but I reminded Bobby that I was not interested in the burlesque theatres until after I had my surgery. Bobby told me that we should go, see a show, and speak with Sam anyway.

I remember when I entered the theatre it was extremely smoky. Everyone smoked back then. The show opened with a big announcement as the drummer tapped out a solo, welcoming everyone to the Follies Burlesk Theatre, the "Home of the Queens of Burlesque." The curtains opened and four girls were dressed in baby doll nighties playing with powder puffs. They powdered each other and blew powder to the audience. The top banana and the straight man did a bit which introduced the first act which was Eve Adams. This sequence of comedy followed by a dancer was the structure of burlesque theatre shows. After a longer comedy bit that included the talking woman, they introduced the co-feature of the week, Eva Wild. Eva was named appropriately as she had a very wild persona and was flashing the audience with her g-string. The comedians did their last schtick and then announced it was "star time". The band played the star's overture song as the emcee from behind the closed main curtain excited the audience with descriptions of the dancer's attributes and her tag line "Forty-eight by the tape. Miss Sally the Shape"!

The curtain opened and Sally paraded across the stage to a sultry song. She peeled off her gloves and dress very gracefully. For her second song she performed bumps and grinds to St. Louis Blues. In her third song she did sexy poses on her prop where she removed her bra and showed the audience her marvelous, enormous breasts. They were forty-eight indeed. She closed with the song "Tequila". She shook her breasts to the music and the audience went wild. The Emcee was shouting over the cheers, "Sally the Shape", "Forty-eight by the tape", "Sally the Shape!" For the curtain call, the emcee announced each person in the show in order of their appearance and that was the end. Some patrons exited the theatre, but many stayed to see the next show.

After the show we walked into Sam Cohen's office. Sam told me I was more beautiful than he thought. He wanted me to start working there within the next three weeks. Sam wanted to eliminate the comics because they'd been around from the beginning and no one was laughing anymore. He wanted to do something different and innovative. Sam wanted the band leader to emcee and to have three good acts followed by the co-feature, an intermission, three more acts, and close with the feature. Sam said that Libby Jones had told him how young, tall, and beautiful I was, and that is why he wanted to meet me. I turned to Bobby and said "I'm not sure I'd be a good co-feature. I have only worked in clubs and I don't think I'm a good act." Bobby told Sam he would let him know my availability. Sam reiterated that he really wanted me to close the first half of his new style of burlesque show.

On the way home I told Bobby that I was really concerned with joining the burlesque show in three weeks as I would have to share a large dressing room with women and work the runway where the men could look up and see my heavy g-strings. After my procedure I no longer had to use the tape but obviously I was still concerned and feeling insecure. Bobby asked me to do it as he had never had connections in the burlesque theatre circuit, and this could open doors for him not to mention for myself. How could I refuse after everything Bobby had done for me?

I went to Bruno's and had him make me two costumes and a fabulous negligee; then to Larry Sittemberg to have two boas created. I figured if I was going to do this, I needed to do it right.

I opened in the Follies for quite a bit of money. The star of the show was Heaven Lee. We had been friends from before but being cast mates made us even closer. I worked at the Follies for a month and during this time, Jess Mack and Dave Cohen came to see me. They called Bobby and offered me a co-feature for the Ohio burlesque circuit. After four weeks at the follies I went to the Ohio Burlesque Circuit as a co-feature with much success.

When I arrived in Toledo, I saw that my photo had the name Marilyn Morr attached to it. I could not believe my eyes. I entered the theatre and the first person I met was a man named, Ed. I introduced myself and then asked, "Why are you using my photo with someone else's name?" He asked me to follow him to an office. I asked the woman in the office about the issue with my photo. She introduced herself as Rose La Rose and said that I was more beautiful than my pictures. I said, "It's not about how beautiful
I am, it's that my photo has a different name." She said she thought Marilyn was a better name than Marinka. I told her, "My name is Marinka and my contract says I am here as Marinka. I don't know who Marilyn Morr is." She shook her head and then called Ed back to the office to show me to the dressing rooms. I told her if I did not hear the name Marinka when I was introduced, I would not go on. That morning at the first show, she introduced me as Marinka Morr.

Rose La Rose was an Italian girl who at age 14 was brought to Minsky by her mother to try and get her a job as a dancer. They offered her the job of ticket taker and eventually she became one of Minsky's dancers. Rose was wild and would flash the audience at a time when no one else was doing that. She soon became a star due to her risqué behavior. She was arrested many times for removing her g-string. In the 1940's that behavior on stage was almost unheard of. In the late 50's, she opened a theatre in Toledo, OH, called The Town Hall. Years later when she lost the lease, she opened the Esquire Theatre in Toledo. Rose was only 59 years old in 1972 when she passed away from breast cancer.

When I finished my show, I was told that I had to wait in the dressing room with everyone else, including   79 the feature, for Miss Rose. When she entered, she began by showing a girl from Chicago her agent photo and asked what happened to her long hair. The girl replied that she cut it because her boyfriend liked short hair. Rose replied, "Well I'm not your boyfriend so for the next show you better figure out a way to have long hair. Otherwise you're going back to Chicago." I felt sorry for the girl so I gave her my extra wig. Rose had a second photo and referred to a girl who had completely shaved. Rose said "I can't see one pubic hair coming out of the g-string. Why did you shave? The girl said, "I like to shave in order to wear this small g-string." Rose replied, "These men see enough bald pussies at home. They don't need to come here to see bald pussies so don't shave the rest of the week." She then asked me if I liked the last name Morr. I told her that I didn't have a last name I was just Marinka. She said well here you're going to be Marinka Morr. She then asked me why I wasn't a feature. She said, "Why is the prettiest girl here not a feature? Look at my feature. She's old already." The feature didn't speak to me for the rest of the week. Rose was such a true character and I really liked her. But every day she would come up and talk to me and I was so afraid that she was going to say something about my heavy g-strings.

One day she asked me again why I was not a feature. I told her that I didn't think I was feature material because I didn't use a prop or have enormous breasts. I told her that I had been a night club act for a few years but had only ever worked in one other burlesque theatre and that I planned on getting married and quitting the business. She offered to call Jess Mack and have him send me to work with her for a few weeks when I finished my circuit. She said she would choreograph and teach me what I needed to work as a feature.

After I finished the Ohio circuit, I went home to stay for a while as I had my date scheduled in December for my surgery. I asked Bobby to have Jess not schedule me back to Toledo until the beginning of February once I had healed from my surgery.

Chapter 11 – Sex Change Operation

Rod took me to the Seven Arts Hospital around 6:30 p.m. on Sunday, December 14, 1969. I had to sign so many documents that it felt like a book. I wasn't even sure what it was that I was signing. I paid the two thousand dollars and gave the receipt to Rod. We had to go to the waiting room and wait for the nurse. When she came for me, Rod hugged me and wished me good luck.

The nurse took me to a private room. She told me to make myself comfortable and to put on the robe. We had to wait for the admitting doctor. She asked me if I was thirsty and I said that I would like to have a glass of water. Shortly after, the doctor arrived with a clip board. He asked me my name and my date of birth. He explained that he would need to perform a complete physical. He listened to my heart and lungs, the nurse returned with my water and the doctor asked her to stay. She needed to be in the room as witness while he examined me. After checking my vitals, the doctor told me to sit on the bed and open my legs. He told the nurse that he didn't see any testicles and that she needed to witness this also. This was very embarrassing for me as no other woman other than my mother had seen my genitals. I asked the doctor why this was so important. He explained that if I had testicles, I would not be able to have the operation as it was illegal for a male to be castrated in the City of New York. In that moment I realized how smart Dr. Prado had been at maneuvering around the law. The doctor ordered an enema and told the nurse that she would need to shave my genitals. He also prescribed a sleeping pill for later that evening and I could only drink juice or have jello. When the doctor left, he wished me "good luck".

Two nurses came in to administer the enema. An hour later, the nurse came back with a different nurse and asked if I had used the bathroom. I told her, I had. They then proceeded to shave my genitals and thoroughly clean me.

They finally left me alone and I began to say a rosary. I had lost track of time and when I asked, the nurse said it was 9:30 p.m. She gave me my sleeping pill and I just relaxed and fell asleep.

Very early the next morning I was awakened. I was only allowed to suck on ice cubes. The nurse cleaned me with Betadine and gave me a new robe. She also changed the bedsheets. Someone came in to transport me to the operation room. I was praying to God for forgiveness. I also asked God that if I was not going to be happy, to let me die during the operation.

I had never seen an operating room before. I saw a room filled with many lights and lots of medical equipment. They transferred me to a gynecology exam type of bed. I had to place my feet in the stirrups, and they proceeded to strap me down by my hands and ankles and then also across my abdomen. The nurse then gave me my IV. Dr. Prado arrived, wished me good morning, and asked me how I was feeling. He then asked the nurse if they were ready. The anesthesiologist put the mask over my face and told me to breathe deep. I went off to paradise.

I woke up and found myself in my room. A nurse was there, she had brought me water and wanted to know if I was thirsty or in pain. I told her I only felt weak. Once again, I was only allowed to have juice, Jello, and chicken broth. I was happy to hear her also mention milkshakes. A little while later, I realized that my mother, my godfather, and Rod were in the room. They could only stay for a short time as I was weak, and the nurse told them that I needed my rest.

The next day when I woke up the nurse brought me a real breakfast consisting of scrambled eggs, toast and coffee. The nurse asked if I had any pain and if I had rested well. She told me that they had to give me a blood transfusion during the surgery, and explained that if I was comfortable, she wouldn't have to adjust the morphine. It wasn't until that moment that I even realized I was getting morphine.

82

Dr. Prado stopped in to check on me and to ask how I was feeling. He also explained to my mother that everything had gone well during the operation. I continued to sleep for most of that day.

On the third day, Dr. Prado came to visit and told me that I needed to get up and move around. He supported me on one side with the nurse on the other. We walked very slowly around the room and to the hallway and eventually back to the bed. I felt a little stronger this day and was interested in watching a little television. The doctor had instructed the nurse to remove the morphine. She explained that if I had pain then she would give me a pill, although I never ended up needing anything for pain. I felt uncomfortable but had no pain.

On the fourth day, Dr. Prado arrived around ten in the morning. He told me I needed to walk the hallways. With their assistance we took off down the hall. He asked how I was feeling and asked if I thought I could stand on my own. I told him I thought I could. He and the nurse let go of my arms and I was fine. He asked if I could walk on my own and I did. Dr. Prado told me I could go home the next day after 2 p.m.

That afternoon, Bobby Colt and his wife Cathy came to visit. I was able to introduce them to my mother and my godfather. They told me that I looked terrific. Later that evening Bruno and Baby came to visit and brought me a package with pink panties.

The next day I woke up and had breakfast. After breakfast, I was able to use the bathroom and walk the hallways. I was a little tired from this. Dr. Prado came to see me around 11a.m. and asked the nurse to close the door. He asked me to sit at the edge of the bed. The nurse placed a pan below me on the floor. Dr. Prado explained that he was removing the packing. There were yards of gauze being removed. There was a burning feeling but not a lot of pain. The nurse brought a mirror and Dr. Prado had me look at his work. He said, "Look at your pussy. I made you a good one." This was like looking at a miracle. I said, "Can I call you daddy, because you have given me a new life?" He just started to laugh. He then lubricated and replaced the gauze inside of me. I was to come to his office the following Monday to have the stitches removed. In the meantime, I was not allowed to bathe or take a shower. I had to have my mother wash my body with water and alcohol.

Rod and my godfather took me to my sister Irene's to convalesce. I spent these few days relaxing and rejoicing in my new self. I had very little pain. When Rod came to take me to see Dr. Prado on Monday, I had a full face of makeup as I was tired of not wearing it.

I went to Dr. Prado's office. He removed the stitches and the packing. He showed me a silicone dildo that he had made for me. He explained that I would have to use it to dilate myself. He lubricated me with vaginal gel and inserted the dildo. This was one of the first moments that I felt pain and was uncomfortable. He explained that I was supposed to do this in the bathtub with warm water two or three times a day for twenty minutes. This was extremely important in order to keep the vagina from closing. I had to do this until I started having sexual intercourse with my boyfriend. He set my next appointment for two weeks, but I was to call if I had any problems.

In the new year, 1970, I went with Rod for my check up with Dr. Prado. He examined me and congratulated me on doing so well. He was able to insert the dildo with ease and cleared me to have sexual intercourse.

When we left the office, we walked to St. Patrick's Cathedral. I lit a few candles and thanked God for everything being successful and for giving me this new life that I had been wanting for so long. We left the cathedral and headed across town to Bobby's office. He was extremely happy to see me and congratulated me on how great I looked. I told him to contact Dave Cohen to book me back into the burlesque circuit. Bobby said it would take a few weeks to arrange it and asked if I would want to work on the weekends around the city. I said that I would like the work and Bobby booked me at the Top Hat that weekend. The following weekend I worked at the 802 Club, and then the next week I worked five days at the Moulin Rouge.

The Moulin Rouge was a beautiful night club located in Staten Island, New York just near the Bayonne Bridge to New Jersey. Bayonne was a very busy port for both cruise ships and cargo. Because the Moulin Rouge was just across the bridge this allowed for a lot of business.

The exotic performed Tuesday through Saturday. Tuesday through Thursday they performed on a small stage at the bar with taped music, and Friday and Saturday in a big room with a band, a comic and a singer. It was a place for couples to enjoy fine dining and dancing on the weekends.

I had worked at the Moulin Rouge a few times on weekends with the Powderpuff Revue. This time I was working as the exotic and of course under the name, Marinka. The staff all recognized me from my Powderpuff days, and I was worried that they were going to cancel me. I was so wrong; they were very excited for me to be there and celebrated me with a bottle of champagne. Even the regular weekend customers were inquiring with the staff and asking, "Hasn't she been here before?" I had become quite the sensation. The owner requested that I stay for the next three weeks. I told Bobby I needed more money and he negotiated an extra one hundred dollars per week. This made me very happy as I knew that I had become a featured name in the industry and I really enjoyed my time there, as the Moulin Rouge was a very beautiful nightclub. Behind my back, the staff from the bartenders to the waiters, were telling the regular customers that I was a sex change.

I needed to have my identifying documentation changed both with immigration and with the courts. I went to Levidow and Levidow, attorneys at law, to facilitate all my paperwork. They said I needed my birth certificate, a letter from Dr. Prado, and a copy of United States residency with my prior name. They also asked what name I was going to adopt. I gave them the name, Maria Arias. The retainer fee was two hundred dollars and the charge for the court papers would be five hundred. They said it would be another five hundred dollars to change the green card and immigration papers. I then decided I would handle the immigration changes myself. Mr. Levidow told me that the court would require that we place an ad in the newspaper for thirty days informing the public that I had a name change. It was enough to place the ad in a small newspaper. He also said there was a possibility that the court may order an inspection by the New York Health Department, and the judge may require me to come to court. Mr. Levidow said this process could take anywhere from three to six months and that he would know more definitively once he filed the papers, which he would do as soon as I had given him the five hundred dollars. Two weeks later I returned with my documentation and the rest of the money I owed him. On the 28th of February 1972, the Supreme Court of New York declared me a female to be henceforth known as Maria Arias.

and stead of the present name, upon complying with the

provisions of Article 6 of the Civil Rights Law and of

this Order, namely,

That this Order be entered and the said Petition

upon which it is granted be filed within ~~twenty (20)~~ Ten (10) days

from the date hereof in the office of the Clerk of the

Supreme Court of the State of New York, County of Queens;

That within twenty (20) days from the date of

entry hereof, a notice shall be published in the

Queens Ledger ~~located at~~

~~and~~ ~~located at~~

A newspaper published in the County of Queens, in substantially

the following form:

Notice is hereby given that an Order entered
by the Supreme Court of the State of New York,
County of Queens, on the ~~21~~ day of March,
1972, bearing Index No. 2220/72, a copy of
which may be examined at the office of the
Clerk, located at the Courthouse, 88-11
Sutphin Boulevard, Jamaica, New York, grants
me the right, effective on the 10 day of
April , 1972, to assume the name of
Maria Arias. My present address is 89-16
178 Street, Jamaica, New York; the date of
my birth is January 6, 1940; the place of
my birth is Oriente Province, Cuba; my present name is Humberto Arias Moreno.

That within forty (40) days after the making of

this Order, proof of such publication by affidavit shall

be filed with the Clerk of the Supreme Court of the State

of New York, County of Queens;

That following the due filing of said Petition and

entry of said Order, as hereinbefore directed, the publication

upon which it is granted be filed within ~~twenty (20)~~ Ten (10) days

from the date hereof in the office of the Clerk of the

Supreme Court of the State of New York, County of Queens;

That within twenty (20) days from the date of

entry hereof, a notice shall be published in the

Queens Ledger ~~located at~~

~~and~~ ~~located at~~

A newspaper published in the County of Queens, in substantially

the following form:

Notice is hereby given that an Order entered
by the Supreme Court of the State of New York,
County of Queens, on the ~~21~~ day of March,
1972, bearing Index No. 2220/72, a copy of
which may be examined at the office of the
Clerk, located at the Courthouse, 88-11
Sutphin Boulevard, Jamaica, New York, grants
me the right, effective on the 10 day of
April , 1972, to assume the name of
Maria Arias. My present address is 89-16
178 Street, Jamaica, New York; the date of
my birth is January 6, 1940; the place of
my birth is Oriente Province, Cuba; my present name is Humberto Arias Moreno.

That within forty (40) days after the making of

this Order, proof of such publication by affidavit shall

be filed with the Clerk of the Supreme Court of the State

of New York, County of Queens;

That following the due filing of said Petition and

entry of said Order, as hereinbefore directed, the publication

---

HARRY BENJAMIN, M.D.
NEW YORK AND SAN FRANCISCO

October 14, 1971

44 East 67th Street
New York, NY 10021
(212) 427-4455

TO WHOM IT MAY CONCERN:

This is to certify that Humberto Arias Moreno, now known
as Maria Moreno Arias, has been a patient at this office
since November 21, 1969, with a diagnosis of transsexualism.

In November and December, 1969, Maria underwent sex reassign-
ment surgery and must now be considered of the female sex, with
appropriate changes in all legal papers.

This patient was last examined by me on October 14, 1971.

Further information concerning this patient can be obtained
through this office, accompanied by the patient's written
consent for release of such information.

Charles L. Ihlenfeld
Charles L. Ihlenfeld, M.D.
Associate,
Harry Benjamin, M.D.

At a Special Term, Part II, of
the Supreme Court of the State
of New York, held in and for the
County of Queens, at the Courthouse, 88-11 Sutphin Blvd.,
Jamaica, New York, on the 28
day of Feb. , 1972.

PRESENT:

HON. Michael A. Castaldi
Justice.
- - - - - - - - - - - - - - - - -X
In the Matter of the Application of:
HUMBERTO ARIAS MORENO
For Permission for a Change of Name to: 2220/72
MARIA ARIAS.
- - - - - - - - - - - - - - - - -X

ON READING AND FILING the Petition of HUMBERTO

ARIAS MORENO, duly verified the 26th day of January, 1972,
duly sworn to January 28, 1972
and the affidavit of DR. CHARLES L. IHLENFELD, and upon

examining a copy of Petitioner's Birth Certificate, and the

translation thereof into the English language, and it

appearing that the Petitioner is requesting that permission

be granted to assume the name of MARIA ARIAS in place and

stead of the present name, and the Court being satisfied

that the said Petition is true, and it appearing from said

petition, and the Court being satisfied that there is no

reasonable objection to the change of name proposed, and

it further appearing that the said Petitioner was born on

January 6, 1940 in Oriente Province, Cuba,

NOW, on motion of LEVIDOW & LEVIDOW, attorneys for

the Petitioner, it is

ORDERED, that the said HUMBERTO ARIAS MORENO, born

January 6, 1940 in Oriente Province, Cuba, be and Petitioner

hereby is authorized to assume the name of MARIA ARIAS in place

87

1970
88

1970

90

1970

1972

1972

OWTIME GOOD SEATS AT BOX OFFICE **NOW**

HELD OVER! 2ND SMASH WEEK!
VALERIE CRAFT ★ **MARINKA**
PLUS
MISS NUDE AMERICA ★ ALL NEW GIRLS

ERS

FOLLIES

NOW!
at the
PUSSY-CAT

Miss Rose La Rose

"A new and different exotic find."
WALTER WINCHELL
N.Y. Mirror

"Premier dynamic ecdysiast."
EARL WILSON
N.Y. Post

1974 on the runway and on the Marquee at the Follies Burlesk in New York.

Rose La Rose my burlesque mentor.

1974 & 1976 the Lobster Trap in Halifax , Nova Scotia

1975 Saints and Sinners

1975

102

1975

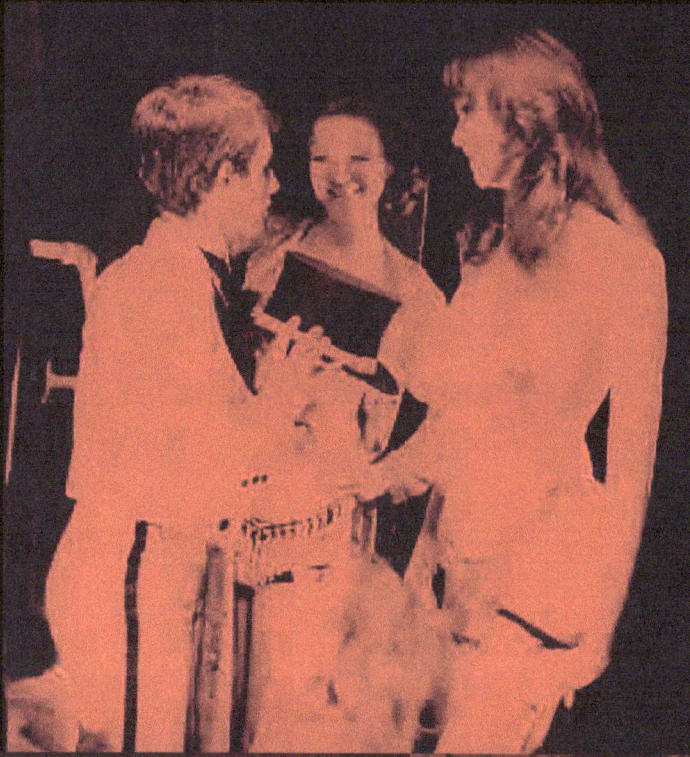

1979 With Bob Fosse and Roy Scheider in "All That Jazz"

Filmschauspielerin zu Gast im St.Galler Nightclub «Tiffany»

Im Monat Mai ist auf der Bühne des Nachtclubs Tiffany in St.Gallen Melani Hunter zu bewundern. Die grosse Attraktion aus den USA, genannt «Busenbomber», wird allabendlich ihre Show präsentieren. – Weltbekannt geworden ist Melani Hunter (unser Farbbild) vor allem durch den Film «All that Jazz». – Daneben ist im Mai-Programm auch Miss Maurren aus dem Fernen Osten absolut sehenswert, welche eine Super-Artisten-und-Akrobatik-Show vorführt. Weitere Künstlerinnen kommen aus Ungarn und Wien. Den Showblock beendet Jeanine aus der Bundesrepublik. – Natürlich wird im Tiffany wie immer grosser Wert auf eine gediegene Atmosphäre gelegt.

MARINKA

MÉLANIE HUNTER

En mai 1980 au CABARET-DANCING
LE PLAZA à Fribourg

l'artiste du film « **All that Jazz** »

MELANIE HUNTER

en compagnie
de 10 danseuses et hôtesses

17-666

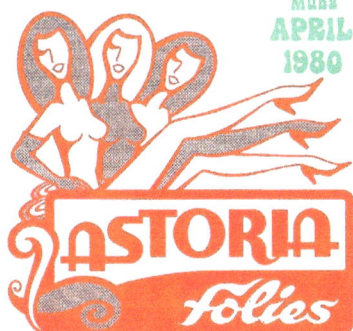

Muba
**APRIL
1980**

ASTORIA folies

**NIGHT CLUB-CABARET
REVUE-BAR-DANCING**

Girls Girls Girls
sexy sexy Girls
in unserem brillanten
MUBA-Programm
mit internationalen
Schönheits-
Tänzerinnen

Sex Erotic Strip-
Revuen

Freie Strasse 52
4051 Basel
Telephon 25 8115

Direktion. Rosmarie Senn

Montag bis Donnerstag, 20.30 bis 02.00 Uhr,
Freitag und Samstag bis 03.00 Uhr geöffnet.
Sonntag geschlossen.

Rosie Sanders

Coffee

Melanie Hunter
Cupa Dandress

Kaly Love

Liliana Contini

DINERS CLUB

AMERICAN EXPRESS CARDS

1980 Melanie Hunter press from Switzerland

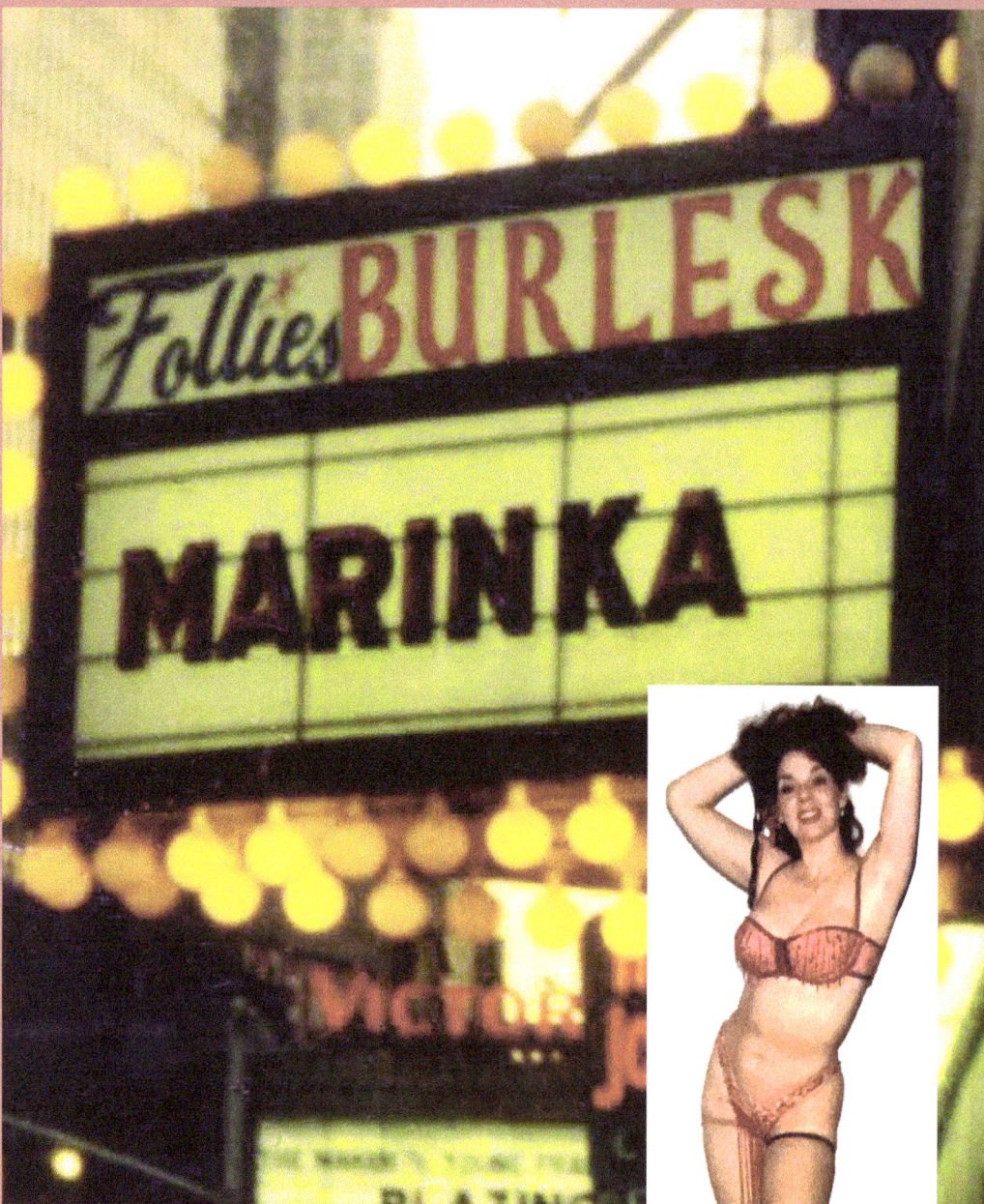

1974 marquee in Times Square

1978 my friend Anita Ventura

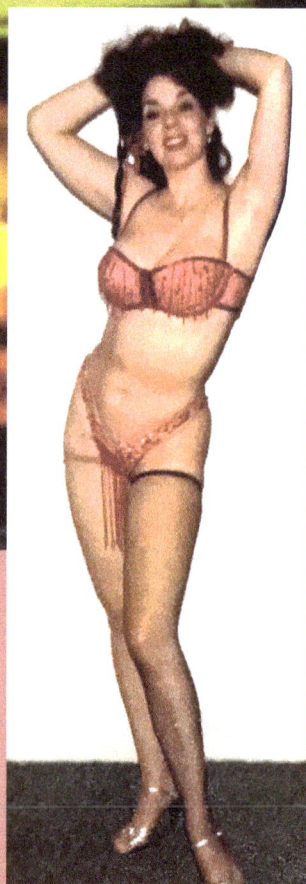

Chapter 12 – Becoming a Burlesque Feature

I returned to Toledo to work with Rose. She and I would work during dinner breaks and in the mornings before the first show. That way we could use the stage to rehearse. She told me that the features were still doing what had been done in the forties. She thought that the old routines needed to go and that we needed to do something new and different. Rose wanted me to use a prop and to go over and bump the curtain. I wasn't interested in bumping the curtain, I didn't see what that would do for me. She said, "It's going to become your signature." I told her that it was not in me and she said "Yes, it is in you. Just imagine you're fucking your boyfriend". She choreographed me to "fuck" the curtain, bump and grind my way back to the center and then as the curtain was closing, I would turn around, grab the right curtain in my right hand and the left curtain in my left hand. I would hold the curtains under my butt and Rose would hit my butt with a spotlight.

After a couple of weeks, the act was polished, and she told Jess Mack to book me as a feature. Rose wanted me to be booked at either the Roxy in Cleveland or Park Theatre in Youngstown. This was important as she wanted to be able to come and see me perform. The Park Theatre had an opening and that was where I did my very first feature performance.

Every feature had an overture song. Rose gave me "Everything's Coming Up Roses" from Gypsy. The band started playing my overture, and the emcee began, "Ladies and Gentlemen, the Park Theatre proudly presents, the feature of the week. She's a new feature making her debut. She's young, she's talented, she's beautiful and a newcomer to the burlesque circuit. She is Marinka, 'Queen of the Amazons'!"

The band began to play "Sophisticated Lady" and the curtains opened. There I was facing a full theatre! I was feeling very nervous yet extremely excited with a thousand thoughts in my head. After my first number when I heard the applause, the high that I felt was so overwhelming that it lasted for thirty-five years.

In my second number, I began to peel part of my costume. I was wearing a creation by designer, Frank Page. It was multiple colors of blue sequins with a psychedelic design, royal blue gloves, and a royal blue ostrich boa. My second number was performed to "Blues in the Night". I removed my gloves and my gown, now with full confidence that I had the audience.

My third number was the prop number and performed to "Nightmare". On the prop, I played and posed in very provocative ways while imagining what I would do to my boyfriend in bed. Getting off the prop, I walked very sexily to the edge of the stage, grabbed the side curtain and performed my signature "fuck the curtains". People were screaming from the audience and I thought to myself, "Rose was right. It did work!".

For my fourth number, "My Heart Belongs to Daddy", I worked the front of the stage bumping and grinding. At the end of the song, I grabbed the right curtain and crossed to grab the left curtain and bring them to center stage. I held the curtains under my butt. The lights went down and the spotlight focused on nothing but my bottom. The emcee was shouting, "Miss Marinka! Miss Marinka!!" The cymbals crashed and I was a feature!

Once I made my feature debut, Bobby was able to negotiate my new fee with Dave Cohen and Jess Mack. I was going to receive six hundred and fifty dollars for each week at the eight theatres in the Ohio circuit. This contract set the standard; I was assured to receive this amount of money as a minimum for any bookings in the future.

Currently in my life everything was going great. I was making a name for myself in my business and I was in such a better place emotionally. I no longer had to worry about being found out! I no longer had to go through the process of hiding in any and all circumstances. I no

112

longer had to deal with the mental anguish of not being complete. I was who I was meant to be. Rod and I could have a sexual relationship. When he penetrated me the very first time, I finally felt like a complete woman and Rod asked me to marry him.

I headed out on the road again. I stopped in Toledo OH, to work for Miss Rose La Rose at the Esquire Burlesque Theatre. When I saw Rose and we talked about everything, she was so thrilled about what was happening in my life and glad to have me there as her featured performer. I continued to find success with each theatre on the tour. I was one of the youngest features on the circuit. I only knew this as it is what people told me. I had not met any of the other features doing the circuit because there was only one feature booked in a theatre at a time.

When the eight weeks ended, I was very tired and returned home. A lot of clubs were reaching out to Bobby to book me and I could not accept the work as they were not able to pay my minimum contract fee. I had to turn down work with Sam at the Silver Slipper. He would not pay that amount of money for a feature in his club. However, he also owned the Plaza Burlesque Theatre in Washington DC where he booked me for a week at my rate. This was the case with most of the clubs. I did not have a lack of work as I was receiving bookings all over the country. This resulted in having to do a lot of traveling and so I then had to become more selective with what bookings I could take.

Chapter 13 – The Catskills

I had been working for Johnny Martinelli and Bobby Colt steadily in club dates, nightclubs and theatres. However, in all this time I never signed an exclusivity contract with either one. I received a phone call from an agent named Joe Williams. He invited me to his office for a meeting and he told me he booked the hotels in the Catskill Mountains. I was familiar with the hotels there as I had worked there a few times with Joey Tone and The Pandora Box. I brought Mr. Williams my photos and publicity and he offered me a contract to perform one show in three different hotels mostly on the weekends. He introduced me to the office staff, and to Mr. Rapp the CEO of the agency, Charles Rapp Enterprises, Inc. Joe explained the details of what I would be paid and what the hotels would expect of me. They offered me a five-year contract for work between Memorial and Labor Day. Mr. Williams told me that I would be working with some very "big name" entertainers. I asked him how he got my name. He told me that Lenny Allen, a well-known comedian that I worked with frequently, had highly recommended me. I was leery of signing a five-year contract, but he reiterated that it was only during the summer season at the Catskills. I told him I would take the contract for my lawyer to look at. He asked if I could go that weekend to the Brown's Hotel and Resort and I told him I would. Mr. Williams told me the clientele was mostly couples and that Lillian Brown required clean, very lady like, and elegant shows from her exotic dancers. They would also be sure to work out a ride with either the singer or the comic for me to travel to and from the show. Once I had my own transportation, I would be given a room to stay. I accepted the booking for that Saturday night at the Brown's.

I told Rod that afternoon about the contract that I had been offered. He couldn't believe it. He was so very happy that I would be able to work nearby. He told me to call Mr. Williams and explain that he would be bringing me to the Browns and to ask for a room. After reviewing the contract, the Lawyer gave me the go ahead as everything was for summer work only at the Catskills.

That Saturday when I arrived at the Brown's, I checked in and went to my room. I went to the nightclub early to get to know the space. I had rehearsal that evening at 7 p.m. and then I was to perform in the late show at midnight. Rod and I went early to listen to the singer and the comedian. We sat at the bar and I introduced myself to the bartender. That night I had a fabulous show. The audience was very well receptive of me.

The next morning when I was checking out, I was told that Lillian Brown wanted to speak to me. I went to see her at her office, and I introduced myself to her. Lillian told me that she wanted me for two Saturdays every month and possibly some extra dates during the week. I really enjoyed that weekend and liked the Catskills, so Rod and I discussed it and decided that it was a good place for me to be working. I called the Charles Rapp agency and accepted the five-year contract.

Joe Williams gave me an immediate schedule. I was to go that Wednesday to the Tamarack Lodge and Friday night to the Gilbert Hotel. The shows were to be a minimum of twenty minutes and no longer than thirty. It was just me with the band and the emcee.

I quickly became the most popular exotic act in the Catskills and all the hotels were requesting me. On busy weekends, I would perform a double. I would perform an early show in one hotel and the late show in another. Whenever there were conventions, I was picking up extra shows as well.

I let Johnny Martinelli and Bobby Colt know about my contract with Charles Rapp in the Catskills. I told them that on my days off I could still be booked for other work. Johnny and Bobby were happy for me and felt that I deserved this break after everything I had been dealing with.

116

I loved working in the Catskills. It was very professional and agents from around the country would go there to scout talent to be booked in places like Las Vegas. The Catskills gave me the opportunity to work with such names as Rodney Dangerfield, Edie Gorme, Alan King, and Debbie Reynolds to mention a few. Working there was a beautiful experience with gorgeous hotels and great food. I really felt like a star. The bands and musicians were great to work with. Most importantly, the love of my life was happy. I accompanied Rod to the Monticello racetrack and people recognized me. They came up to say hello and congratulated me on my work. I was actually a little famous.

The guests at the hotels would have dance classes in the morning. They would learn the cha cha, rumba, conga line and the mambo. In the evening they could practice their newly learned dances with the band in the nightclub.

After working in every one of the hotels from the Nevely to the Concord, I found that my favorite was the Gilbert Hotel. I was booked there frequently. The dance instructor at the Gilbert was Fabiola, and the bartender was Syd. Fabiola and Syd helped to make my stay at the Gilbert a fabulous time. I also liked to work at the Singer Hotel. My show there was an early show at 9pm. It was a very elegant exclusive place and due to my show being early I could often pick up a second show.

The hotels in the Catskills were frequented by mostly rich upper-class Jewish people from the New York area. The Catskills were where they went for their summer retreat. Some families would stay the entire summer and the husbands would stay in the city for work and return to the Catskills for the weekends. I can't explain how wonderful it was to work in an environment where everyone was just there to have a good time and enjoy their vacations. They were the best audiences ever. They always made sure to let me know how much they appreciated me.

In my shows, a good eight to ten minutes was dedicated to audience participation. I used to go down into the audience, teasing the husbands and the women would all go crazy trying to get me to go to their husband next. I would bring one guy up on stage and if he wasn't very tall, my breast would be right in his face. I would joke to the audience, "dancing with boobs in the eyes". The audience would always laugh. I would take the gentleman's shirt off and have him sit down in a chair on stage. Then I would take his necktie and wrap it around my hips with a knot placed right on top of my g-string. I would have the man untie it with his teeth while I was bumping and grinding. Every time he would miss the knot with his teeth the audience would go crazy laughing. Sometimes there would be a wise guy who would make me work a little harder and sometimes there would be conservative ones who would need help untying the knot. Of course, I made sure to ask the audience to applaud them with some funny quip like "Come on. Give him the clap."

For the next number I would wear a negligee and perform to the bluesy classic "Summertime". I would parade a little and get another guest to join me on stage. I would have them peel my stockings and while they were busy with this task, I would writhe in the chair and give them a hard-sexy time. Once my guests returned to the audience, I would continue to remove the rest of my clothing, pick up a boa and do a little closing number to a Latin rhythm.

One morning I entered the hotel cafeteria for breakfast before my return home to New York, and a woman came up to me and thanked me as she continued to explain that she and her husband went "back to romance" after watching my show. That made me feel good.

While working in the Catskillls, I felt wonderful. I felt like a professional performer who was finally respected. It was such a step up from the smoky clubs and the burlesque theatres. I was also working alongside of some of the biggest names in show business. The exotic dancer may have been the lowest entertainer on the ladder, but in the Catskills, you were treated as a professional entertainer.

Chapter 14 - Married to Rod

Rodney Melvin Portnoy and I were married on August 6, 1973 at the justice of the peace. The only family member present to act as my witness at the ceremony was my niece, Aixa Martin. After the ceremony, we went to dinner at a first-class restaurant with the rest of the members of our families. We could not go on a proper honeymoon as I was still working in the Catskills. Instead we had a "Broadway Honeymoon". This consisted of going to see every Broadway show that we wished. We saw The King and I and Gypsy among many others. We would also go out to a fine dining dinner with each show. We were waiting to take a real honeymoon after Labor Day. However, that never happened because I was contracted to head out immediately back to the burlesque circuit.

Rod and I took out a larger apartment in the same building in which we had been living. It was located at 399 Ocean Parkway, in Brooklyn. We spent a lot of money decorating and making the place ours. We were a very happy couple and I felt blessed. I was married to the man that I loved, and he was very supportive of my career.

Within a few months I noticed that Rod was using my money to feed his gambling habit. I complained to his mother, Sydell. She said, "Maria, watch your money. I never had anything as my husband was always a degenerate gambler and he took Rod to the racetrack when he was only six years old." She said, "Since you have to shake your tootsie to earn it, you need to keep your eye on it." Even after finding out about my missing funds, I was still in denial about how bad it was. I loved Rod more than my own life. Rod was my hero. He was the most special person in my life. In my eyes, Rod could never do anything wrong.

I was working all the time, but we never had a penny. Rod was gambling our money on the horses. Whenever

I said anything to him, Rod would always convince me that we would have a beautiful home and lots of money, and that I would be able to stop working. When he won, he would take me to the best places and treat me like the most special person. We were so in love that we were oblivious to everything else. Rod would ask me what I wanted and whatever I said he would give me. He taught me how to drive and bought me a brand-new Coupe de Ville Cadillac. Rod said, "This is how much I love you." He told me he would get me the large house that I wanted too. At this time, Rod made me feel like a million dollars. When he would lose, there were obviously no gifts, he would get really depressed, and I couldn't help him.

Rod's friends were, at the very least, interesting characters. When Rod's friend Ari was getting married to his fiancée Rene, Rod was in the wedding party. Rene called and asked me not to wear a sequin gown to her wedding. She didn't want me looking like a stripper not to mention showing her up on her day. Rod's friend Mel was waiting for me outside the burlesque house one evening. I asked him what he was doing. He said, "Rod sent me to pick you up." On the drive home he was trying to hit on me. I told Rod and Rod informed me that he had never told Mel to pick me up. That incident caused the two of them to have a distant relationship for a while.

I was lucky that Rod's family loved me, but his friends just saw me as a tramp that they could all try to get their way with. Rod was always on my side and would tell his friends that I was an entertainer and demanded respect for me.

That fall I was out on the road working various bookings and sending the money home. I was gone for about eight weeks and when I returned home, instead of having several thousand dollars in my account I found that the account was bankrupt. We were now going to have to survive on the money Rod earned driving taxi because he had spent my earnings at the track on a "long shot" and lost!

After a long discussion with him, I asked him to see a

psychiatrist. This was the first real argument we had. Rod insisted that there was nothing wrong with him and that he had no need to see a psychiatrist. He explained that he just loves the horses and one day he was going to beat them, and I would be a happy woman in a big mansion with my own horses in the back yard. He just went on. I would not wish this kind of a relationship on my worst enemy. Living with a gambler was horrible as they have two different personalities.

Once things calmed down between us, we had another long discussion. Rod convinced me to agree to purchasing a taxicab medallion. In New York, taxi cabs had to work under a medallion. It could be privately or corporate owned. If Rod had his own, he could work whenever he wanted and keep the money. He would also be able to rent his cab along with the medallion to work when he wasn't. He would receive $200 per shift from anyone renting his medallion. He explained that we would be able to have enough income in the future when I quit dancing. He also agreed that if I bought the medallion, he would see a psychiatrist. Even though a medallion cost twenty-five thousand dollars, I was happy to agree. This helped us to have more earnings coming into the household, which was wonderful, but the consequences of this were that Rod was never home.

At this time, my agent, Joe Williams, called and asked me to dinner. He said that he had a hotel owner from Lebanon that wanted to meet some of us performers. At dinner, Lorie Green, Aura Moon, and myself were introduced to the owners of the Crazy Horse Hotel and Salon in Beirut Lebanon. The contract they offered to me was for three months with round trip airfare and hotel accommodations. The contract was for $170 net per day plus commissions for champagne and caviar. I asked Joe Williams how I could get out of the contract with the Catskills. He told me that Lebanon was a good deal for the agency and that they were able to get me excused from the Catskills for that one summer.

Lebanon was a very exotic country. The first thing

the owner told us when we arrived, was that under no circumstances were we to go out by ourselves. He would provide us with an escort. There were multiple European shows playing at the time. Beirut was known as the Paris of the middle east. The royalty from other countries traveled to Beirut as they were not able to enjoy such entertainment in their country. In any given day you could find yourself drinking champagne with a prince or a king from any of the Arab countries.

One evening the maître' d' of the club asked me to a table that had requested me. When I came to the table there were several men. I was introduced to one of the gentlemen, his name was, Mohammad; his favorite drink was Cristal, we drank several bottles and had caviar while having conversation. Mohammad was very wonderful to me and told me that he would have to be leaving after my next performance. He thanked me and told me he would leave some gifts for me. After my act, the maître d' gave me a bottle of Cristal and two hundred dollars as a tip from the Shah of Iran. Not to mention the hundreds of dollars I had made in commission from his table. Being in Beirut was a wonderful experience.

When I returned home, I had ten thousand dollars in my purse. I gave it to my mother to put away for me. Rod asked me what I did in Lebanon and I told him I was just having a good time. I had sent home money each month while I was there. I told him that I bought a lot of things and that's where my money went. Rod never found out about the money I brought home.

We became very argumentative and I became very sad and depressed. I would drive to Coney Island and just sit and look at the ocean as I had when I first met Rod. This time I was there to contemplate suicide. I really felt I couldn't live without Rod. Rod told me that he felt that we were not good for each other. He said that he hated to see me unhappy, that he missed the vibrant, excited, happy girl that I was before we were married. He didn't like what was happening to us. I told him that he would need to choose between myself and the horses.

122

I started to take every job possible to be away from the house. When Rod was home, I was usually sleeping, and we rarely saw each other. We no longer had the beautiful relationship or friendship that we had always cherished. The evening before I was to open in Dayton, Ohio, Rod and I had an argument. On opening morning during the show, I walked off the runway and fell into the crowd. I had a huge sprain to my left ankle. I had to cancel my whole tour and return home in a wheelchair.

Rod arrived home to find me there with my sprained ankle and we began to argue once again. He repeated that he felt that we were no longer good for each other and I once again asked him to choose between me and the horses. Rod said, "I love you, but I can live without you. I cannot live without the horses."

I went to do a show at the Gilbert Hotel. This was when there was a gas shortage. While driving on route 17 I pulled into a gas station and got in line for gas. The attendant was a man with a hook for his right hand. He came to the window and told me that he was not selling anymore gas that day. I was in full makeup with a low-cut sweater and he said, "If you're nice to me maybe I will sell you some gas." I thought he meant a good tip and when I asked him what he wanted from me, he replied, "a little blow job". I told him that he was mistaken and explained that I was an entertainer at the Gilbert Hotel and not a hooker. I tried to drive away, but he put his hook on the hood of my car near the windshield and I was afraid I would hit him if I moved. I yelled for help, but no one responded. I happened to keep a large wooden stick in my car. I grabbed it and poked him with it. I yelled for him to get away from my car and then I drove away.

When I arrived at the Gilbert, I told Syd the bartender that I needed a double scotch. I explained what happened to me. After the show was over that night, I went home and told Rod, but then I didn't think much about it after that. A few days later, the South Falsburg police department called. When I answered the phone, the officer told me that he had a warrant for my arrest. I asked him what it was for. He asked me if I had an altercation at a gas station on route 17. I said yes and told him what happened. He then informed me that the gas station attendant was pressing charges and was accusing me of trying to physically attack him because he wouldn't sell me gas. The officer told me that I needed to come to their station, and I agreed. Rod went with me and they photographed me and took my fingerprints. They explained that I would receive a letter letting me know when the court date would be. Because of this I couldn't leave town until I received the news of the court date. I went to the court with Rod and told my story to the judge. He believed me and threw the case out.

Then it was time to head back out on the road. I told Rod that when I returned, I would like for him to no longer be living there. He respected my wishes and was gone when I came home.

I received a suit for divorce that listed me as the defendant and the reason being mental cruelty. I went immediately to see my lawyer and he was able to get the suit reversed so that I was the plaintiff and I sued Rod under cruel and inhuman treatment. The divorce became final on March 21, 1975.

Portrait by A. Thibault De Navarre

1987 in Jerusalum and Egypt

1977 Marinka and Tony
1985 Armando Mendez
and Marinka
1983 Marinka and Tony at
Maxim's Restaurant, Paris
1987 Roberto V. Consolazio

1992 Mara, Marinka and Valentino,

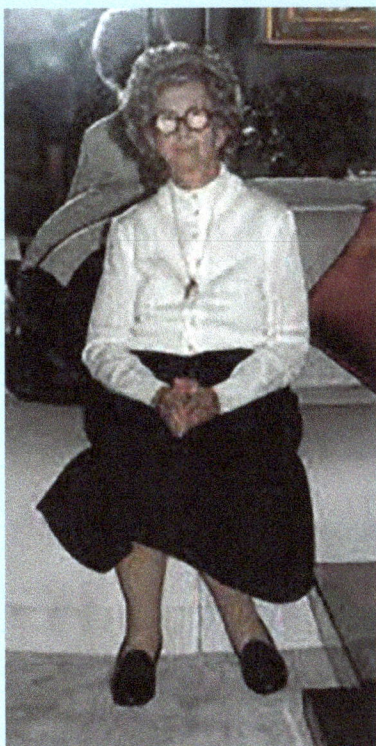

1983 My Mother in my home in Edison, NJ
1989 My sister, Mercedes with Coco

1990 performing with
Tony Randall and Jack
Klugman
at the
Roseland Ballroom.

1991 With David Letterman backstage of the Lyceum Theatre

1985

1993 Carmen Flores and Lola Flores, and Paquita Rico- Sevilla Fair

1987 Powderpuff Reunion
with Chi Chi LaVerne, Felix de Masi, Tish and Frankie Quin

1987 Felix De Masi at "Don't Tell Mama's" New York
1990 Nefertiti

2011 Performing at The Burlesque Hall of Fame
photographed by Ed Barnes

2013
Burlesque Hall of Fame
photo by Derek Jackson

2016 Susie Cardee, Sylvia Rivera and Marinka

2009 Performing at The Burlesque Hall of Fame photographed by Ed Barnes

Chapter 15 – Playing the Field

Christmas 1974 was one of my worst ever. I was unhappy and alone. I did have my work and my two best friends, Anita Ventura and Rita Bennet. I was dating anyone that I was interested in and who could afford my tastes. They would take me out to the best restaurants and discotheques. I was booked into a new club named after the proprietor, Sue Rendezvous, located in Brownsville, NY.

The club was very attractive with several topless dancers working seven days a week, and one exotic would work Wednesday through Saturday. That week I was hired to be the featured exotic. Sue was a very glamorous Italian lady that had that old-time class. She was always dressed impeccably, and many customers would come to the club just see Sue and have a drink with her. One evening she introduced me to one of these customers. His name was Lou Smith.

Lou was an older, classy man who would soon be taking me to the very best places all over New York. I really liked Lou; our favorite restaurant supper club was Jimmy Weston. We also enjoyed the Chateau Madrid. Lou loved to eat the chicken livers over white rice, and I would drink champagne and eat caviar. It was with Lou Smith that I experienced my first orgasm.

Lou would buy me Fogal pantyhose, which were the most expensive nylons that were only available in the high-end department stores. Lou was also the man who bought me my very first diamond ring and would always send a limousine to pick me up at my home. If we had too much to drink, he would go to his car to get his suit luggage that included a clean suit, shirt, tie, underwear and shoes. This way he would be ready for work the next day if he stayed with me at my place. Needless to say, we were taking limos all over New York. It was with Lou that I visited Jack Parr's home in Brownsville and was invited to parties with the Governor and other politicians around Westchester County, New York. Lou and I dated from late 1974 until the spring of 1975. I can only imagine what life I might have led if I had married him as he had asked.

I was featuring in the Follies Burlesk in New York when I received a note backstage from my friend, Armando saying he had a friend he wanted me to meet. That morning I was introduced to the artist, Armand Thibault De Navarre. The three of us went out for a quick lunch during my break. Armand told me that he was looking for a model to do a collection of the ladies of the golden age of Hollywood. When he saw me on stage wearing my beautiful white fox, he was fascinated with me. He offered me fifty dollars an hour to pose for him or he would give me a self-portrait. I chose to receive a self-portrait. After lunch they accompanied me back to the theatre and within a couple of weeks I began posing for Armand.

I would go to Armand's studio almost daily. Each time he would have a photo of the movie star that he wanted to paint. The canvas was ready, and he would pose me in the position that he wanted. Sometimes he would use different accessories. Armand would draw my face on the canvas and then he would later paint the movie star's face over the sketch of me. This is a very old technique for creating portraits.

At the end of the project I posed for my own painting, but after receiving my official divorce papers in the mail, I came to the studio and wasn't myself. Armand asked me if I didn't feel well and I explained that I was sad. He told me to sit and he put a shawl around me. I assumed he was continuing to work on my self-portrait.

When my portrait was complete, I asked Armand to take me to the place he used to have his portraits framed. I needed his help making color and design choices. When I arrived, he presented me with two portraits. He painted one the way he saw me on stage, and the second was from that very sad day. He told me he needed to

144

capture the sadness in my face. Armand was so generous that he also gave me a portrait that he created from a photo I had showed him of Rod. His collection of twelve movie stars of the Golden Age of Hollywood were displayed and sold in a hotel in Manhattan. I invited my friends to a party for the unveiling of my portraits. Armand and I remained friends until his death.

I was booked in a show at the San Regis Hotel in Manhattan. After my show, I was introduced to Hanns Wolters by Joe Carroll, the bandleader and my agent for that club date. Mr. Wolters said that he was very impressed with my show and wanted to know if I would be interested in working in Europe. I told him that I was, but that I was still contracted in the Catskills for the whole summer. He gave me his card and I went to see him to bring my photos, etc. He explained that contracts in Europe were for a full month at a time. I told him I could be available after Labor Day, but he said I would have to wait until the new year as booking in Europe was different. They wanted to book people six months in advance, and he would need time to send my photos to the agents that he worked with in multiple European countries. The process would take a little while.

Within a few months Mr. Wolters had responses from multiple agents in Europe. He was sending me to Switzerland as that was the place with the best money. He had received four one-month long contracts from four different cities in Switzerland. I was to begin my European experience on June 1st, 1976.

I signed the contracts and began to prepare for my trip to Europe. I called my designer, Bruno Le Fantastique, to order two costumes. Bruno did some sketches and came up with the ideas for my tiger and zebra costumes. I absolutely loved it as I had asked for something based on the animal kingdom. The tiger gown had one sleeve and used three colors of bugle beads, gold, orange and black. Each color of the tiger print was beaded with the coordinating color of beads. He also created the fan, which was designed to be the face of the tiger surrounded by extra-long pheasant feathers. The zebra gown was made from four separate pieces put together to look like a gown. It consisted of the bra, panties, an under bust corset that went down to the hips followed by a long skirt with a zipper and a slit all the way down the left leg. The zebra gown was created in white and black velvet by cutting the two materials and piecing them together to create the pattern of a zebra. The white section was done in silver bugle beads and the black velvet was left intact. Bruno also made me the most gorgeous pink negligee gown with ostrich feathers all the way around it. We went to lunch and discussed the specifics. I wrote him a large check as this was the biggest investment I had made for costumes.

I then went to see Larry Sittemberg to have him create the biggest, most gorgeous boa possible. It was to be eleven plies of cock feathers and eight feet long. Larry also made me a hat to go with my zebra gown. It was black velvet and had three layers of black cock feathers around the brim of the hat so that it looked like feathers raining down.

By December 1975 the gowns were ready, and I contacted my photographer, James J. Kriezmann to have new photos taken in my beautiful new costumes. Photographers were just beginning to use color for their photo shoots. It was expensive as it was a new and more difficult process for not only developing the photos but also how to do the shoot effectively. This session produced my first professional photos ever in color. When I sent the agents my photos, they were amazed.

By January, I received all my Swiss contracts. I took them to the immigration department to ask for a reentry permit. The United States would issue this type of permit to persons who were permanent residents of the United States, but who did not have a passport from their country of origin and/or had not been able to receive their naturalization papers. Due to my sex change my application for citizenship had been delayed for a few years. Whenever I asked, I was always told they were
146

"working on it". Immigration had a law requiring proof of "good moral character". I knew that my sex change had something to do with holding up the process. This time they told me to wait to see if I received my naturalization by April 1st and if not, then they would give me a reentry permit.

My five-year contract had expired, and I went to the Charles Rapp agency to let them know that I would not be able to appear in the Catskills that summer because I would be in Europe. They were very understanding and congratulated me but were still wishing I could have worked for them.

Chapter 16 - Switzerland

June 1st, 1976, I opened at the Moulin Rouge in Geneva. The cabaret was decorated like La Belle Epoque in red and gold with a beautiful round stage. The tables surrounded the stage and were covered in red tablecloths and the chairs were upholstered in red velvet and gold. The walls were decorated with posters of can can dancers. It was a small club but had a very elegant elite atmosphere with an attractive cigarette girl who sold both tobacco products and perfumes. Along with the champagne they served caviar, smoked salmon, and a cold roast beef platter. The club was in the historic bohemian district of Geneva called the Paqui.

In Europe mixing was referred to as consummation. This was a practice in every European club. I found all the dancers to be very friendly, but I became close with Marlene, an English exotic. One evening the maître d' escorted us to a table. Prince Ali and Prince Samir were two brothers from the middle east who had requested us. They offered us whatever we wanted so I asked for my favorite champagne. They stayed for several days and had dinner with us every evening. Prince Ali bought me my very first Louis Vuitton bag. This liaison with the brothers made Marlene and I very good friends and we remained close.

My sister, Mercedes was pregnant and I anxiously awaited news of the birth. I called to check on both her and my mother. Mercedes told me that she had given birth to a baby boy whom she named Henry. She asked me if I wanted to baptize him and become his godmother. I accepted with joy in my heart. I was so pleased that she had chosen me. I told her we would do this as soon as I returned home.

One evening the maître d' called me to meet a gentleman named Frederick Haas, a German banker doing business in Geneva. For us, it was love at first sight.

He would only be there for the next two nights. He would pick me up at the Pension de Artiste, where I resided. We would go to a fancy dinner and then he would accompany me to the cabaret, and we would spend the evening drinking champagne. He asked me where I would be the following month when my engagement at the Moulin Rouge ended. I was going to Zurich next and he promised to come and see me. By the end of the month when I finished in Geneva, I had received an education in French champagne, and I knew by then that my favorite champagne was Louis Roederer Blanc de Blancs.

On July 1st I bought myself a first-class ticket on the train from Geneva to Zurich. I would spend the next month performing in La Puce Cabaret. The cabaret was in Paradeplatz on the first floor of the building Borse. The Borse is the international financial center of Zurich. Paradeplatz was filled with Swiss banks and just looking at them made me feel rich. La Puce had a large square stage that would double as a dance floor. On the side was a round bar with a barmaid named Marcelle Smith. Marcelle and I began a friendship that lasted until her death. The owner, Mr. Kearney, had studied in New York. He spoke English very well and was happy to have an American in the club. We would sit and discuss the days when he was a young man at Colombia University.

I was staying at the Im Park Hotel when Frederick came to see me. He didn't like me having a single room, so he upgraded it to a suite. We began to have a love affair and Fredrick was extremely generous with me. In those days, there was a French fashion designer, Leonard. Frederick took me to the famous boutique, Grieder, and bought me two of his gowns. He also took me to Bahnhofstrasse where every brand name of Swiss watches had its own showroom to buy me my first Swiss watch. Fredrick and I were completely in love. I wish that month of July would have never ended.

On August 1st I took a taxi and all my luggage to Basel. I spent that month working in Clara Variete which was a complex of restaurants, cabarets, theatres, and coffee shop terraces located on Claraplatz. The artists lived upstairs in Clara Variete. The nightclub was on the first floor with a large round stage with tables and chairs. The second floor was a mezzanine with a huge square bar. The mezzanine was reserved for the VIP clientele. This is where the dancers and customers would meet and mix. The show at the Clara was a variety show that included a circus act, a band with a singer, an emcee, and three exotics. Living upstairs made it very convenient as we only had to come down the elevator to be at the club.

Frederick was calling me every day and came to visit me while I was in Basel. We had a great visit. One afternoon at lunch he told me that he had spoken to his family about me. He wanted me to go to Hamburg when I was finished with my bookings. He explained that he was very much in love with me and wanted to introduce me to his family. He said he wanted to marry me and felt that maybe since I was in my mid-thirties it was time for me to have a child. I felt that Frederick deserved to be told the truth about me. I waited until we returned to my apartment. I told him that I was not able to bear children and that I had been born a boy. He started to cry and wanted me to tell him that it was not true. "It's not a joke, this is the truth." I said. He wanted to know why I hadn't told him. I told him, "I can't go through life with a sign on my head saying, 'I used to be a boy'. I never thought we were going to get serious. I thought this would be a wonderful affair and that I would go back to America and never see you again." He packed his valise and left. I stayed in the room completely devastated. This had never happened to me and I never even thought about it happening, but I now realized this was something that I was going to have to deal with. Frederick returned to the room and told me he loved me very much and that he wanted to think of it as a dream. He took the train and left, and I called out sick from the club. I thought that would be the last I would ever hear from Frederick.

I continued working at the Clara. One evening I was called to a table and was introduced to Mr. and Mrs.

Werner Baiter. They were international agents based in Basel. They both used to perform in the circus but worked now as agents. Mr. Baiter offered to have me go to different European countries to work, like Holland, Italy and Spain. I told him he would have to contact my agent, Hanns Wolters, in New York. The Baiters were most excited to be able to book me in these other countries. At the end of August, I received a phone call from Frederick. He wanted to know where I would be working next. I said, "I'm going to Lugano." He said he would come visit me there.

I left Basel by train on the first of September. It was a good four-hour ride. Lugano is the Miami Beach of Switzerland. It is on Lake Lugano which borders Italy and is in the part of Switzerland known as the Swiss Italian.

I was booked in the Casino Kursaal. The club, as usual, was very nice with a stage and tables and chairs with a bar. They had a six-piece band and there was dancing between shows. I worked there with another dancer from Austria, Helga. The management was very relaxed and would even allow us to go to the casino between shows. We started work at 10pm so our afternoons were free to relax and sightsee.

I had been in Lugano for about a week when Frederick came to see me. Even though I was heartbroken over this relationship I allowed him to visit. We had an incredible time in Lugano. He was always a gentleman and treated me incredibly well. Frederick said that I would always be in his heart. If it wasn't for having to respect his family, he wouldn't care one way or the other. I knew that this would be the last time I would ever spend with him. The day he left was the first time I realized that my concept of "love" being the strongest emotion was not true. There are other situations such as family, duty, and work that come into play in a relationship. This was not one person leaving another. This was two people who don't want to let go, saying goodbye forever.

I worked my contract in Lugano through the 26th of

September. I had arranged with the director to finish that day since I had to re-enter the United States by September 30th. I flew home to New York on September 27th having had an amazing experience in Switzerland which I was very happy for, but I also came home with a broken heart.

Chapter 17 - Meeting Tony

When I arrived home from Switzerland, my friend, Leslie Tulips, called me to see if I could do a show for a retirement party in Elizabeth NJ. I had a show that evening in the Catskills, but this event was earlier and wouldn't conflict, so I told her I would as the money was good.

When I arrived at the venue, I was greeted by a tall handsome man who looked like a football player. He said, "Leslie was right. You are beautiful!" His name was Tony. The restaurant was filled with men. Tony introduced me to David who was running the show and showed me to the lady's room, which was being used as our dressing room. I entered the lady's room and saw my two very good friends, Susan Cummings and Anita Ventura. Anita replaced Bettie Page as the pinup model in the underground and dated many members of the Mafia. They were drinking champagne and smoking pot. Leslie offered some to me. I told her that there was already enough in the air to get me high. Leslie told me that she was opening and that I would close the show. Tony asked what I would like to drink and offered me some food. I told him I didn't eat before I perform but that I would have a double scotch on the rocks. I asked him if the show was going to start soon as I needed to leave by 9:30 to get to my next show in the Catskills. Tony offered to drive me there if I would like. That way I could relax, and he could get there in an hour and a half. The show was running behind as the men were long winded in their roasting of the retiree. Meanwhile, Tony kept bringing me drinks and we chatted. I really liked Tony and again he offered to take me to the Catskills. He said I could relax, and we could get to know each other better. I accepted but told him that I needed to leave my car at the Palisades so that when we came back, I could easily cross the George Washington bridge to head back to Brooklyn.

Tony was driving a white Continental Mark IV. On the way to the Catskills Tony told me his full name was Antony Da Silva. He was twenty-seven years old and divorced. He said he worked as a warehouse manager for Bristol Meyers in Elizabeth NJ. Before we knew it, we arrived at the Gilbert Hotel.

We went straight to the club and after I put my costume in the dressing room, Tony and I sat at the bar listening to the comedian. I introduced Tony to the bartenders, and we had a drink. He was ecstatic over how nice the place was and how well everyone treated me. When the comedian finished his act, the emcee announced, "It's time for coffee and cake and to put the children to bed. The next show will be our late show with the exotic, Marinka." The emcee came over and told me that I had over an hour as he would announce me around 12:30 a.m. All the musicians came over to say hello to me on their break. Eventually I made my way to my dressing room to get ready. After I finished my show and came back to sit with Tony at the bar, he could not believe the kind of dancer I was. The show I had just performed was not the same as the one I did at the retirement party. He was very enamored. Syd the bartender said that we should get a room as we had been drinking a lot. I told Tony the room was for "sleeping". He agreed. The next morning after breakfast we headed back to the city and I gave him my phone number. Tony asked me to dinner on Tuesday to celebrate his birthday. I told Tony that I had received my letter regarding my citizenship and that I had to go that day to swear my oath.

At dinner on Tuesday, I told Tony that I was so happy to finally be an American citizen. He asked me if I had to work on Saturday. I told him I didn't, so he asked me to keep it open. He wanted to take me to Windows of the World. This was a restaurant on the 106th and 107th floors of the north tower of the World Trade Center, with a magnificent view of the city.

I was wearing a very beautiful and unique red silk dress. Tony wore a fabulous blue suit. After a wonderful

156

dinner we headed to Studio 54 to go dancing. When we arrived, there was a line from the door all the way down to Broadway. I told Tony that we didn't have to wait in line as the bouncers knew me and I had carte blanche. We walked right in. Tony was becoming more and more mesmerized by me.

Tony would stop by to visit me almost every day. Whenever he left, he managed to "forget" something of his. When he visited, he brought with him some of his favorite music albums, which varied from Simon & Garfunkel to Kiss. Some I liked and some I didn't. We spent the next few weeks really getting to know each other.

My doggie, Chelo, was getting older and I needed to go to Halifax, Nova Scotia. I asked Tony if he would take care of Chelo. He said he would. He called me every day while I was away and when I returned Tony had moved into my apartment. I was so stunned and couldn't believe that he had taken advantage of the situation. I asked him what he was doing and why he thought he should move in with me. He said "Well we are in love and I'm serious about my feelings for you. We are going to be together forever." I was very uneasy with this situation. I was finally a citizen and had planned to get my American passport as I had returned home with six months of contracts to go back to Europe. I had been considering giving up my Brooklyn apartment. I really liked Tony, but I didn't know him well enough to be living with him. I knew his name and that he was twenty-seven and divorced. I let Tony stay but I told him that I was not yet committed to the relationship.

Living with Tony was nice. He was very amorous toward me and would do the shopping and cook for me. I learned over time to like him a lot. On Thanksgiving I brought Tony to my sister, Mercedes, for dinner. He met my mother and my godmother, Irene. They all liked him. I asked my mother for advice on my situation. She told me to follow my heart. She said, "You don't always find love, but you can find work." I decided to have a serious talk with Tony.

One evening, I started a discussion with Tony about my having to decide between staying in New York or going to Europe where I had the opportunity to make a lot of money and visit many beautiful new places. Tony said that our love was forever and the real thing. Europe was only temporary. Tony did not even consider the idea of me going. It was the first time that he told me that once we were married, he didn't want me travelling. After my experience with Frederick, I decided to tell Tony everything about me. I did not want to give up career opportunities for a relationship that may not last. It was then that I told Tony, that I needed to tell him who I really was and that he may not love me after all. Tony did not want to hear anything about my past. I insisted that it was very personal and that he needed to know and to hear it from me. I said, "I want you to know that I had a sex change operation a while back." He looked blankly at me. I said, "It's true. I had the sex change seven years ago". Tony said, "Stop joking around, I don't like those kinds of jokes." I insisted that it was the truth. I told him that if after knowing my past, he still loved me, I would marry him and not go to Europe. He asked me again if I would swear that it was true. I said "Yes, I have no reason to make this up." Tony threw his glass against the wall and became very aggressive and was very "insulted". Tony headed into the bedroom and packed his clothes in his valise. He told me that he didn't have room in his life for that. "You're lucky I love you otherwise you'd be dead!", he shouted. As he headed out, he said he'd be back to get the rest of his belongings and slammed the door.

Two days later, Tony called. He had not returned to pick up his belongings. He asked me if I was okay. I said, "Yes. I'm okay." He told me he would see me that weekend. The following day the doorbell rang and there was a delivery man with a dozen red roses. The card read, "Pick you up at seven for dinner. Love you, Tony." It was at this moment that I realized how much I really liked him. I picked up Chelo and we danced around the room

158

while I chanted "Daddy's back!"

During dinner Tony told me he loved me, and he didn't want me to go away. He also said he had something to tell me. "I have a son," he said. I asked him why he didn't tell me. He didn't think it was important but since I had been honest with him, he felt he should be honest also. I asked about his son, and what his name was. He told me his name was Antony Da Silva III, but he didn't want to talk about him tonight.

Tony came back to the apartment a few days later. When he arrived, he brought with him a most perfect blue spruce Christmas Tree. I thought it was fake until I smelled it because it was perfect. He asked how long it had been since I had a Christmas tree. I told him not since I lived with my sister. We bought ornaments and spent the weekend decorating the tree.

On Sunday, Tony told me that he wanted me to give Rod his portrait. He wasn't comfortable having it in the apartment. I didn't want to give it to Rod so I called my friend, Eva Novak, to ask if she would keep the portrait for me.

I called Hanns Wolters to let him know that I would not be opening in Madrid in a month. I told him that I really needed to give my relationship with Tony a try. Mr. Wolters advised me to get a letter from my doctor stating that I was under extreme emotional stress and wouldn't be able to travel. I got the letter and gave it to him. I recommended to Mr. Wolters a friend of mine to fulfill my contracts. Her name was Ezi Rider, and she went to Europe instead of me.

Tony and I had a wonderful holiday season. We hosted a Christmas party that year. I was also able to spend the holidays with my mother. After the new year, Tony was trying to talk me into moving to New Jersey. I couldn't see myself living there after living in New York. Jersey seemed like a different country. He insisted that it was not only expensive to commute for work but also, he had to spend two hours with traffic and pay the tolls. I agreed to move to Jersey but only to North Jersey. We found an apartment in North Bergen in Boulevard East in the Stonehenge building. The apartment overlooked the New York skyline. We moved in July 1st, 1977.

Shortly after we moved in, Tony brought Little Tony home with him for a visit. I couldn't believe how young he was. I asked how old he was, and Tony said, "He's two." Little Tony was an adorable little boy and I felt so bad for him growing up without his father. I asked Tony why he didn't go back to his family. Tony told me it was because he did not love Myrta.

Once we moved to Jersey, Tony started to be very demanding about me not working in show business. We argued daily about it. Eventually, he talked me into going to learn how to do cosmetic merchandising. I went to a six-week course and was hired at Claremont Chemist in their cosmetic department. I found the work very boring. The only good thing was that the owner of the pharmacy, Marty Raiman, would sit and talk during the slow time. I will always remember that Marty would tell me, "Let it pass. If you're patient enough, it will pass."

After a few months living in the Stonehenge apartment, I met Myrta. I liked her. She was a very nice, lovely woman who was quite pretty. I also found out that she and Tony were still married. I demanded that Tony tell me the truth. Tony admitted that they were not divorced but that he would be getting the divorce that year. He told me that he left Myrta when he met me. I told him to get his clothes and go back to her.

I quit working at Claremont's. I thanked Marty for everything and told him that I had a friend that I could train to do my work. I brought Eva and she learned my duties and Marty hired her.

I told Tony that he had no right to tell me what to do with my life when he was still married. Even if he wanted to marry me, he couldn't. I repeatedly told him to go back to Myrta and Little Tony, but he refused.

Baby Martell called to tell me that Bruno was sick and had been admitted to the St. Clare Hospital. I went to see him, and Bruno told me they were running tests because

160

they didn't know what was wrong. They thought that it might be a cancer of the liver. I told him I would come see him again in a few days. When I returned Bruno was very weak and tired of having so many tests done. They still didn't know what was wrong and he felt that he'd feel better at home. He told me he was craving a glass of Chianti. I left the hospital and found a nearby bar. The bartender sold me a bottle of Chianti and at my request, two wine glasses. He was very nice and opened the bottle for me too. I put it in my purse and took it back to Bruno's room. We drank the Chianti and Bruno was happy. He was discussing his favorite subject, fashion. Rene Del Rio called me the next morning to tell me that Bruno had passed. To this day his cause of death is listed as unknown.

Agents were calling me to work both in and out of town. Ann Corio called me to go on the road to work at all her dinner theatres. Tony was furious that I was taking this work. Dick Richard asked me to work at Acra Manor on Sundays through Labor Day and I also went back to working Saturdays at the Gilbert Hotel. The only time I was home was Monday and Tuesday.

That whole summer was nothing but daily arguments in the house. Tony came home one day with all the papers to show me that he hired a lawyer and started the divorce proceedings from Myrta. That next Christmas Tony gave me a blackglama mink coat and the certificate of divorce. We had a very nice holiday season. On New Year's Eve, I was booked in Rodney Dangerfield's nightclub. Tony was there with me and we rang in 1978 with the promise of marriage.

My mother had been living with my sister, Mercedes. She had not been getting along with her son-in-law. To alleviate the problem, I asked my mother to come live with me and brought her home. Tony was fine with this, but we needed a two-bedroom apartment. There wasn't one available in the Stonehenge building, so we found a new place that had two bedrooms and once again in Boulevard East overlooking the New York skyline.

Most weekends we had Little Tony staying with us. My mother became very fond of him. We were like a real family with three generations, spending time together and making pleasant memories. Tony asked me to marry him and gave me a two-carat marquise cut diamond ring. This was a very happy time and I accepted. We went to the municipal court of North Bergen, New Jersey on March 15th, 1979 and were married. My mother, Maria Moreno, and my nephew, Alphonso Verdu were there as witnesses and to share in our moment. Following the ceremony, we had lunch with my mother and Alphonso and then took a flight to Acapulco, Mexico for our honeymoon. The week that Tony and I spent together was a most beautiful experience.

When we returned home from the honeymoon, all the sweetness Tony had shown to me was gone. He started to try to hammer home the idea of me staying home and spending time with my mother. He was really against me working at all. We decided to investigate buying a home. Interest rates were high and if we had bought a home, we would have been house poor. I told Tony that I would only work the Catskills, Poconos, local hotel club dates and the burlesque theatres. That way he didn't have to worry about or be jealous of me spending time in clubs. Because my shows were all local Tony would be able to drive me and be there with me. I told Tony this was how it was going to be. I didn't want to be home with nothing to do except count pennies. If I worked, we would have a large supplement to his salary. I told him before we were married that I was not going to quit working and that I really wanted to buy a home.

Martinelli called me and asked me to return to the Top Hat. It was just a few miles from the JFK airport. The Top Hat was an elegant Italian restaurant with delicious food and they also had entertainment. It was the type of restaurant where people celebrated birthdays, anniversaries, and divorces. They had a band and dancing between performances. It was a respectable, fine restaurant which on Fridays and Saturdays would have a singer, comedian and an exotic for two shows each evening. Wednesday and Thursday, I would perform alone to taped music for two shows each night. It was on one of those Wednesdays that Bob Fosse showed up with a film crew to have dinner.

After my show I was requested at their table. They wanted to meet me and congratulate me. Bob was very enthusiastic toward me and told me he was going to cast me in a film. Before the night ended, I gave him my business card so that he would be able to contact me in the future. Within a few weeks, the casting agency called to have me come into their office.

Chapter 18 – All That Jazz

I went to New York and signed a contract with the casting agency. They gave me the script for the movie. Later that day I met with Bob Fosse for lunch. We hit it off immediately and began a very good friendship that led to romance.

Two weeks later we began filming. First in Astoria Studios and later at Purchase University in Purchase, New York. Purchase University had a round auditorium that the production lined with aluminum paper to create a mirrored effect. I shared the dressing room with Leland Palmer, Ann Reinking, Rita Bennett, and Erzsebet Foldi. The dressing room was always a lot of fun and we all got along beautifully. We had to work late hours and by the time the bus would return us to New York it was around 9pm.

Every day was an argument with Tony. He wanted to know why I had to be gone so long and could not be home for dinner. I told him he could read my contract and that it's just the way it was. He couldn't understand it and I began to lose respect for him. John, one of the dancers from the film, taught me some yoga relaxation exercises to help me relieve the stress from home.

During one of our breaks on the set, Roy Scheider asked me if he could get me a drink. We began to have a conversation and I found him very attractive. From that point on, whenever we had a break together, we would sit and talk. He asked me for my phone number. I told him I would give it to him but that I was married and if a man answered he would need to hang up. He told me that he was married too and said, "So we are both married". We went on like this throughout the filming.

By mid-December the filming had wrapped, and the casting agent called me to discuss my being in Playboy regarding the movie. Playboy had run two articles, one about the film and one about sex in 1980 films. I had to sign a release for my photos to Playboy and received my check for the publications. The film opened to enormous success. I went to the theatre to see the film with Tony, he was very proud of me.

Roy called me and we had our first private meeting in the Warwick Hotel in Manhattan. He always had my favorite champagne and caviar waiting for me when I arrived at the suite. We spent many beautiful afternoons together. I felt guilty that I was cheating on Tony, but I felt alive and appreciated when I was with Roy. Roy felt guilty that he could not take me out to dinner or shopping so he would leave an envelope with money on top of the night table.

With the release of the film, agents were getting calls from theatres and nightclubs to book me. When the film was showing in a town the clubs were wanting to pay for my appearance and were willing to pay well. I received a lot of very well-paying contracts at the time and Tony began to relax because I was making a lot of extra money. With the success of the film, we were able to save enough money to make plans to buy our dream home.

While filming the movie, a casting director named Sylvia Fay was on the set. Bob introduced me to her, and she began to send me on casting calls after the filming was finished. She got me to do a "walk on" in "Brewster's Millions" with Richard Pryor, and in "Sentimental Journey" which starred Jaclyn Smith. She also sent me to do "extra" work in the film "The Cotton Club" and many others.

I asked Sylvia when she was going to send me for more substantial roles with a speaking part? Sylvia confessed to me that the word had got out that I was a sex change. She said that Bob Fosse wanted to help me but every time she sent my information to the producers, they didn't want to cast me in principle parts because of the sex change. The producers felt that the American people were not ready for a transgender woman in film or television, but Sylvia guaranteed me that she could find me plenty of extra work. I told her that I was a performer and had been in

166

show business for more than twenty years. I said I was an actor and a screen actors guild actor and if all she could offer me was small extra roles because the public wasn't ready for me then I would step aside and go back to where I belonged, in the burlesque houses. This made me feel so terrible for many reasons. A fine bunch of hypocrites though; some of those same directors who didn't want to cast me in speaking roles wanted me in the dark on their "casting couch".

Chapter 19 - Returning to Switzerland

Hanns Wolters called. He told me that the clubs in Switzerland were willing to pay me whatever I wanted, if I would return to perform there. Tony and I made a deal that I could go to Switzerland but for no more than three months at a time. Before I left for Switzerland, Tony bought me an apricot colored toy poodle. It was only two months old. Tony named him Rusty and he went with me to keep me company. Rusty kept me company for the next nine years.

At the same time, Tony got a new job with a British company. He was to oversee the imports from England. This gave him the opportunity for travel to London. It worked out well as it was only an hour flight from Geneva to London. It allowed us to spend time together while I was gone. We had a lot of good times together in London. I even saw the London cast of Evita with Tony. This was generally a happy time for us.

One evening, Tony called to tell me that our apartment had burned. He told me not to worry and that my mother was okay. She was in the hospital for observation. My mother had left a pot on the stove while watching her novella programs and forgot about it. I lost all my family memorabilia. It was a complete mess. My mother went back to live with my sister, Mercedes and Tony went to live with his sister, Alice. I was to be home in six weeks, so I asked Tony to wait for me to begin looking for a place. When I returned, Tony had found a monthly rental as a temporary place while we searched together for a house to buy.

We found a new housing complex in Edison, New Jersey. I chose a split-level model to be built on a half-acre corner lot located on Melissa Court. Construction would not be completed until December which was about four months away. We made the down payment and signed all the documents. The closing was set for December 1st.

Tony went back to his sister's and I returned to Switzerland for the next four months, hoping to return the next time to my brand-new beautiful home.

In December, we closed on the house and moved in with very little furniture. Only the bedroom set had been saved from the fire. We purchased brand new furniture for the family room, and the two extra bedrooms for my mother and Little Tony. I also purchased a temporary dining set. I took my time choosing the dining and living room furniture until I found what I really wanted. Christmas of 1980 was spent in our own home.

I went back once again to Switzerland in February of 1981. I opened in the Maxim's Cabaret in Geneva. The Maxim was the most beautiful cabaret in Geneva. It looked like something you only saw in films of the 40's. It was exquisite. The stage was on the second floor where the dressing rooms were also located. When it was time for my act, I would enter the stage and the stage would be lowered down to the first floor in front of the audience.

The Maxim was known for its oil rich Arab clientele and extensive high-end menu which included caviar and pheasant fricassee. They always had an assortment of entertainment which included comedians, singers, variety acts and two of the best exotics. The Maxim had classy customer service as it was frequented by some of the richest people in the world. The ladies were required to wear a gown to mix with the customers and only upon request. The Maxim was open from ten in the evening until four in the morning. It was there at the Maxim that I met Alain Delon, one of Europe's most prominent actors and screen sex symbols from the 1960s. Each evening you would meet VIPs, actors and other celebrities as it was the most exclusive cabaret in Geneva.

From Geneva, I went to Lausanne to the Cabaret Le Brummell. Lausanne at the time was the home of the Olympic Headquarters and the city where Co Co Chanel is buried. Lausanne was also the city where the Spanish Royalty lived in exile during the reign of Franco. It was a very cultured old city with gorgeous architecture and old-world charm. I always felt luxurious in this cabaret with its velvet lined booths and candle lit tables. It was there in the cabaret that I met and had an affair with the famous author of "le Pays de Lausanne", Jean-Pierre Laubscher. If I had been single, I would have married him.

With the enormous success that I had at the Cabaret Le Brummell, the owner, Madame Bossier, asked me to return to play at the cabaret the following September and October and for every year after. This was the time of year that Lausanne hosted the international film festival.

The following September when I returned to the Cabaret, I was introduced to a man at his request by the maître d', Paul. He told me his name was Baron da Sytha. Baron shouted as I approached the table, "Gloria Divina Regina of my heart." He was the most important artist in the entire region. He adored me from our first meeting and asked me to pose for his collection that was to be exhibited at the Hotel De Ville in Geneva. I attended the exhibition and it was an enormous success. Baron was madly in love with me and asked for my hand in marriage. Another moment in my life where I wished I had been single.

While I had so many opportunities to travel and perform around Europe, my career was really taking off and I was experiencing the most success of my professional career, my personal life was greatly declining. Tony was very demanding of me. He wanted me to travel as little as possible. He blamed me for the situation of needing my extra money to help pay for expenses since purchasing the house. I therefore had to travel, and Tony was lonely. While I traveled, I purchased many beautiful houseware items for my home. I bought beautiful embroidered linens, porcelain Lladro art pieces, and crystal stemware. One of my favorite purchases was a set of glassware from Murano. It was made of glass with amethyst handles. I designed our house to be a showplace.

Tony would visit me in Europe and each visit was wonderful and full of exciting new experiences. Tony never had any complaints. But when vacation was over, that all changed. I was making enough money for Tony to travel with me if that would have helped save my marriage. I offered to have my mother live with my sister and he could come with me. I was willing to do that, but Tony wouldn't have it. Even though he didn't make as much money as I did, he had to keep his job. His machismo would not allow him to let me support him. This was so important to him that he would rather fight constantly and put me down for what I did for work than to swallow a little pride and save our marriage. Tony and I had made an agreement that I needed to work until the house was paid for, but Tony wasn't adhering to the agreement. All these fights and disagreements were killing our love for each other and our marriage.

I was supposed to return home after Le Brummell, but I was offered to work from December 1st through the 22nd at the Mocambo in Bern, the capital of Switzerland. The Mocambo was one of the most exclusive cabarets in Switzerland and was frequented by dignitaries from countries all over the world.

I was scheduled to finish at Le Brummell on October 27th. I knew that Tony had always wanted to visit Paris so I spoke with my agent about opening at the ABC Cabaret in Neuchatel on November the 3rd which would give me five days to spend with Tony in Paris. Tony flew direct to Paris and I took the train from Lausanne. I had made reservations at the Hotel De Vendome. We had a beautiful suite and spent our evenings going to see all the Parisian shows. On the last evening we had dinner at the world famous, Maxim. When we left Paris, we were extremely happy. It was a very successful vacation. I then returned to Switzerland to finish my work.

I arrived home on Christmas Eve. We went out for a quiet dinner with my mother and spent the next day at Tony's sister's. I was home until the following February when I returned to Switzerland and stayed until June. I came home for the summer but upon my return I found that Tony had changed. He was not amorous and very cold to me.

I wanted to finish the landscaping to complete the house, but Tony would not help and wanted nothing more to do with anything regarding the house. For the rest of the year, I travelled back and forth to Switzerland and things with Tony remained cold.

That November when I returned home for the holidays, I wanted to organize a party. I paid no attention to Tony's attitude and began to make my preparations. I invited our family and neighbors and we all enjoyed a spectacular Christmas dinner. Tony was friendly with everyone except me. It was very noticeable to my guests.

Tony would always make plans with me to do something special for New Year's Eve. This year he was barely speaking to me so there were no plans. I decided to cook a nice dinner and Tony sat and ate with me and my mom. He just sat there with a straight face. He was nice to my mother but would not pay any attention to me. My mother and I were watching the ball drop on TV. I had opened a bottle of champagne as was my family tradition to enjoy with grapes. Tony didn't want any and after the ball dropped on his way to bed, he said to me, "Don't you get enough of that champagne where you work?" There were no "Happy New Year" wishes between us.

Every year right after the new year, Tony would always make plans for my birthday. This year he didn't mention it. I didn't mention it either. On my birthday I planned on just staying in. That day Tony came home from work and asked if I was ready to go to dinner. I wanted to say no, but I also wanted to try to work things out before I would have to leave again at the end of the month.

In the car, Tony was not talking. I was doing all the talking. He took me to an Italian restaurant and continued to not say much. He made sure that I did not enjoy my birthday. After dinner, we returned home, and Tony went straight to our bedroom without saying a word. That was when I decided that I would sleep in the extra bedroom, that there was no room for me in our bed.

It was time for me to return to Switzerland. I had my bags packed and was waiting for Tony to come from work to take me to the airport. He showed up at the last minute and asked if I was ready. The entire ride from Edison to JFK, Tony wouldn't say anything. I kept asking him what was wrong and each time I asked he said "Nothing." and turned up the radio. When we arrived at Swiss Air, before I was even out of the car, Tony had my luggage out of the trunk and thrown on to the sidewalk. Then he drove away. I felt like my heart had been stabbed with a knife. I composed myself and asked a sky cap to help me with my luggage. I called my sister Mercedes and told her that she would need to check up on my mother more frequently, as my marriage was over. I spent the entire flight contemplating what I was going to do with my life. By now the stewardesses knew me well as I had taken this flight multiple times. They asked me if I was okay and could tell I wasn't myself. They brought me a lot of champagne on that flight.

I was to open February 1st at the Casita Cabaret. That evening I met the most beautiful person that I had ever known. She was a dancer from Spain and her name was, Mara. I had never had as much in common with any girlfriend as I did her. She was from Seville and Mara and myself, along with my mother, became the best of friends. When I would call home, Mara would have wonderful conversations with my mom. Meeting her at that time in my life when I had so much sorrow was a blessing. Every night when we finished work, Mara would play videos of Concha Piquer, Estrellita Castro and Lola Flores, Spanish singers that I knew from my childhood. She was so amazed that I knew who they were. At the end of February, I had to leave for St. Gallen, but I was contracted to return in April for the Mustermesse. I knew I would see Mara then.

This entire time I was emotionally stressed and didn't want to accept that my marriage was over. I would always call home to talk with my mother when I knew Tony wouldn't be there. My plans were to return home on June 1st but I had to return early because I had been having problems with the silicone in my breasts and had to have

174

cortisone injections while I was working. When I arrived at JFK, I took a limousine to my home in Edison only to find that Tony had moved out the night before.

I asked my mother what he had taken with him. She said that he had taken all his clothes. I also found that he had taken my Cadillac. I told my mother to get dressed because we were going out to eat. On the way, I dropped into the New Brunswick Courthouse and asked for an order of protection against my husband. I explained that he had abandoned the household and was very aggressive. They granted me the order. After dinner I went to Tony's sister Alice's to drop off a copy of the order and a copy to the Edison Police Department. I also kept a copy in my purse.

The next day I called Century 21 to come look at my house and put it up for sale. I gave the agent Tony's phone number and asked the agent to get Tony's signature on the paperwork. I also called my lawyer, Jay Zinewsky, to start divorce proceedings. A week later, Tony called me. Tony asked if we could pick up the pieces. He asked it in a very cold way and never apologized. I told him, "I don't have any pieces to pick up." Tony offered to let me buy him out of the house. I asked him what would make him think that I wanted to live in Edison. I only moved there because it's where he wanted to live.

Shortly after, I had gone to Yonkers, NY with my mother and my friend, Nina Niles to see Dr. Morrison about the issues with my breasts. I didn't like what he had to say and how he said it, so I decided not to have him treat me. Upon returning home, I saw that every light in my house was on. I made my mother stay in the car while I checked it out. I went inside and yelled for Tony as I assumed that he was there. I didn't find anyone in the house, but everything upstairs had been tossed from my dressers and closets. I called the police and they found a broken window in the basement. The police surmised that it was probably neighborhood teenagers. Whoever it was got away with a lot of expensive diamond jewelry and ten thousand dollars in cash.

I got the name from a friend, of a Dr. Tippet who worked in Las Vegas. I called to make an appointment but found out that he was now working in San Antonio, TX. What I didn't know at the time was that the reason he had moved was because Nevada had suspended his license. I spoke with his nurse and after explaining everything that was happening with my breasts and my symptoms, she let me speak directly to the doctor. He told me he could remove the silicone and replace it with implants. He would charge me ten thousand dollars. Ingrid, his nurse, explained that I would need to stay for a minimum of seven days until the stitches were removed. She recommended the motel next door for me to stay in.

I decided to have the surgery while I was waiting for my house to sell and for my divorce to go through. I made the arrangements and headed to San Antonio. I went to the doctor's office and had planned on having the procedure the next day. After talking to him he told me he could do it right then. His nurse gave me an injection and before I knew it, I was on the operating table.

After the operation I could hear them talking but I could not yet speak. The two of them were moving the operation table through the back door and into their van. They were concerned with what they were going to do if I died. They took me to their home as his nurse was also his wife. Once we arrived, I was able to finally speak. They and their two teenage boys took care of me for the next three days. The doctor told me that he was very scared that I was not going to wake up from the anesthesia. They brought me to my hotel, and I was still very weak and only left my room when it was time to eat. I was finally able to have my stitches removed and headed home to New Jersey.

A few weeks later, a doctor from the Kennedy Center bought my house. My lawyer called to tell me that he wanted me to come to his office so he could distribute the checks from the sale of the house to myself and Tony. Tony also had to hand over the keys to my Cadillac in person. Tony was already there when I arrived. He was
176

wearing a pair of dark glasses from behind which I could see tears. He never said a word to me. That was the last day that I ever saw Tony.

Chapter 20 – Union City New Jersey

After the closing of my house, I needed a place to live. My sister Mercedes' husband, Enrique, was renovating a building on Kennedy Blvd. in Union City. The building housed his business on the first floor and had two apartments on both the second and third floors. Mercedes and Enrique were going to live on the second floor, and they offered me my choice of apartment. I chose the other apartment on the second floor so that my mother would be close to my sister and that Mercedes could look after her when I was traveling.

The renovations were not going to be complete until the summer of 1985. I took my furnishings, decorations, and paintings and put them in storage. My mother went to live with Mercedes, and I went to stay with my friend, Armando Mendez, until the beginning of the new year.

We celebrated Christmas that year with just the family. I was very sad because all my dreams had flown out the window. I thanked God that I had my mother and my two sisters along with my nephews and nieces to support me. Otherwise I'm not sure how I would have got through it.

In mid-January, I returned to Switzerland to work at Club Barbarella in Interlaken. Interlaken is one of the most gorgeous places in the Swiss Alps. It was a ski resort and I had a lot of fun working there.

Mara and I had a reunion when we worked together again that April at the Casita Bar in Basel for the Mustermesse. We took a trip together to Spain where we met my mother at Barajas Airport, and spent the month travelling and visiting friends. At the end of May I put my mother on the plane back to New York and I flew back to Zurich to work once again at the Maxim.

While I was staying with Armando, we made plans to take a trip to Paris when I finished my contract at the Maxim. I had reserved a suite at my favorite hotel, Hotel De Vendome. Armando met me there. It was the beginning of one of the most beautiful vacations I have ever had.

We visited the Louvre and Notre Dame Cathedral. We both had been to Versailles before but wanted to visit it once more. We also visited the Palais Garnier Opera House and saw the opera, Roberto el Diablo. We rented a Mercedes Benz and travelled to the French countryside, stopping in different cities until we reached Nice.

In Nice we stayed in the legendary Hotel Negresco. While we were there, we took a day trip to Monte Carlo. We visited the Monte Carlo Palace where Princess Grace had lived. Armando and I also visited the Monaco Cemetery. I wanted to see Josephine Baker's grave and to place some flowers for her.

We spent a few more days in Nice before driving back to Paris. Armando was an intellectual and wanted to visit the library at Sorbonne University. He was fascinated with their antique collection of books. We also visited the Pere Lachaise Cemetery to see the tombs of our favorite French writer Honore de Balzac and favorite Irish writer Oscar Wilde. That evening we went to the Moulin Rouge to drink champagne and watch the can can dancers.

Armando surprised me with the news that the next day we were going to visit Maria Felix. Armando had written to her to let her know that he would be visiting Paris. Armando called her and she said that she would receive us. When we arrived at her fabulous apartment in the late afternoon, her personal assistant met us at the door and showed us into the salon. As I entered, I was fascinated with the gallery of Maria's portraits. Her home was decorated in the style of Louis XIV and full of portraits by her companion, Antoine Tzapoff. It was pure beauty and luxury. Armando and I presented her with a beautiful bouquet of flowers. She offered us champagne and we had a toast. I reminded her that we had met before in 1964 but that I did not look the same. She looked straight at me and told me that she recognized me when she looked at my eyes. It was only a short visit but talking to her was a treasure that I will always keep in my heart.

Armando flew back to New York and I went back to Zurich. It was the most glamorous vacation I have ever had.

I returned from Europe at the beginning of November and stayed a few weeks with Armando until the furnishings were delivered to my apartment in Union City. My mother and I moved in and I spent my time decorating my new place. I went to New York to visit my designer, Felix De Masi and to order a new gown. When I returned home, I had a note from my sister. My mother was in St. Mary's Hospital. I spent the next few days in the hospital with her. She had suffered a stroke and they were having her do therapy. A couple of weeks later she was able to go home but there was still a scare of future strokes.

New Year's I was working a few shows. Shortly after the new year, I woke up one evening and heard that something was not right with my mother. I called my sister and the paramedics. They took her back to St. Mary's. She had another stroke that was worse than the last one. The doctor told me that I would only be able to take my mother home if I had around the clock nursing. He did suggest that in her condition it would be best to place her in a nursing home. The thought of a nursing home gave me the chills. After discussing it with my sisters, we realized that even if we spent all our savings, we would only be able to keep her at home for a short period of time. My mother's stroke had left her completely paralyzed on the left side of her body. She needed assistance with all daily functions. My sister Mercedes and I found a place called Hudson Manor in North Bergen, New Jersey.

Hudson Manor overlooked the Hudson river. It was the best place in the North Jersey area. They had a private room available so we accepted it and transferred my mother to Hudson Manor. We moved my mother in and I got an apartment on Walker St. in Fairview. That way I could go see her every day. I would help bathe her and do laundry for her. My sister would visit her in the evenings. Working out of town was no longer a possibility.

Dick Richard called me to give me an offer to be the star of his show, Dick Richard's World of Burlesque. I was happy for the offer as I had always got along with Dick and his wife, Toni Carroll. Toni and I had been friends for a long time. Dick and Toni were no longer partnering due to Dick's age, so she had a new dance partner, Sebastian, and now went by the name of Jessica. The revue consisted of an adagio partner dance, a top banana, Rex Owen, a straight man, Dick Drew, an exotic dancer, Heaven Lee and me as the star exotic. We had club dates and weekend work from Connecticut to New Jersey. I was working all the time.

Chapter 21 - Meeting Bobby

Johnny Martinelli called to ask me to do a retirement party in the World Famous, Peter Luger Steakhouse. I accepted the job and when I arrived at the restaurant, the maître d' took me to a private dressing room. My appearance was supposed to be a surprise. The host of the party offered me food and drink. I asked for Moet Chandon! After dinner, they did the roast and at this point I didn't know who was in the room. I did my show which included audience participation and had some fun with the retiree. The men were giving me $50 tips and I had doubled my fee in tips. This was a retirement party for Merrill Lynch.

Once I had changed and was waiting to leave, a very nice gentleman came to see me and introduced himself as Bobby. He asked if I had time to have a drink with him. He wanted to take me to Mr. Wong's in Brooklyn. I accepted his offer and we went for dinner and drinks. He was a very respectable man. I offered to drive him home as he did not drive. I was very impressed when we approached Hiker Heights Brooklyn. Hiker Heights was a neighborhood that was notorious for beautiful mansions that belonged to the mafia. When I saw where he lived, I asked him if he was in the Mob. He assured me that neither he nor his family had ever been involved in that type of business.

After that evening, Bobby called me every night and we started dating. From the very beginning Bobby was very generous to me. He knew how hard I had to work to pay for my mother's nursing home and to take care of myself. He told me that he admired me very much and explained to me that he lived with his mother and would not marry while she was alive.

Bobby always loved good food and we went to the very best French and Italian restaurants. Bobby was always first class. He would sometimes accompany me if I had a show in the Catskills. He loved watching me dance. After only a few months of dating, Bobby took me to meet his mother, Rose and see his home. I was also invited to his brother Richard and his wife Gloria's home. Shortly after, I had met the extended family. Even though he would not marry me we had a very serious relationship. I was his official girlfriend.

Bobby told me to pick out what car I wanted, and he would buy it for me. I saw an advertisement for the new Buick Le Sabre, so I told Bobby that's what I wanted, and Bobby paid for it in cash. He would take me shopping whenever I wanted at places like Saks Fifth Avenue and Bergdorf Goodman in New York. Bobby liked me to be well dressed as he was always dressed impeccably well. Whenever we could spend New Year's Eve together, he would take me to the party at the Waldorf Astoria with Guy Lombardo leading the band. It was a very exquisite party.

Bobby often told me that he loved me. I told him that I knew that he loved me, but I wasn't good enough for him. Bobby never wanted to hear anything about my past. He was only interested in who I was at the time. He was always very complimentary and a real gentleman. It's one of the reasons that I fell in love with him. I felt like my marriages were failures, but I knew Bobby and I could have had an incredible marriage. Even though he clearly loved me, and we had a fantastic relationship he still would not propose while his mother was alive.

My life was very full at that time. I was still helping to take care of my mother during the day, working in the evenings and spending time with Bobby whenever I could.

Bobby would always give me great Christmas presents. He would say, "Whatever you want." He had given me so many gifts that I started to tell him that I didn't want anything, and he could give me whatever he wanted. So, he would give me a card with a few thousand dollars inside. Bobby paid for everything in cash. I told him he needed an American Express Card because I was very uncomfortable with him carrying so much cash in his pocket. Shortly after, Bobby had his first credit card.

While I was dating Bobby, I told him, "Since I'm not your wife, I do not have to be faithful to you." Bobby couldn't understand the idea of that.

I went back once more to work for the Saints and Sinners. The New Jersey chapter would put on a large dinner with a high-priced plate. They would invite a sports star, or a politician as the "fall guy" and the money would be sent to charities. I was a favorite of the Saints and Sinners, so I worked with them often. After the dinner, they would hold a VIP party. At one of these events, I met a man named Michael.

I was very attracted to Michael. He gave me his card and started taking me out to dinner. He was a married man with no children. Michael fell in love with me and I found him very desirable, so we began a love affair. Michael would send me the most beautiful bouquet of flowers every Tuesday. That was our day to meet and spend a nice afternoon together and dinner that evening. He also treated me very well and gave me a lot of nice gifts.

That Christmas, he gave me a card with a lot of money. I had been seeing Michael for a few months when his wife found the florist charges on the credit card. Our Tuesday afternoons had to come to an end. The last day I spent with him, he told me that if it wasn't for being involved in a family business he would divorce and marry me. He said, "Maybe one day I will come back."

I would often find myself comparing Bobby to Michael. But one day I realized that Bobby was the real winner. He was always there for me and never asked anything of me. He allowed me the freedom to do and to be whatever I wanted. No man ever gave me as much material happiness as Bobby. I accepted Bobby for who he was and that we would never marry. I knew he loved me as much as he was capable. He could only idolize one woman at a time.

Bobby and I went to dinner at my favorite Italian

restaurant, Ponte Vecchio, in Brooklyn, New York and after a couple of bottles of wine, I told him, "I accept how you feel and what you need but I feel like a kept woman." He didn't feel that way, but I explained to him that was exactly what I was. I told him that I needed him to buy me a condo in Manhattan so that if anything happened to him, I would always have a place to live. Bobby said, "No." He assured me that I had nothing to worry about and that if anything ever happened to him, I would know how much he loved me. In other words, I was in his will. Bobby thought maybe I was too stressed and asked where I might want to go on a vacation. I told him I wanted to go back to Egypt one more time. Bobby of course would not accompany me due to taking care of his mother. I asked my sister, Mercedes if she would be able to help my mother during the mornings also. She agreed. I went for two weeks to Egypt and Israel.

I had been fascinated with Egypt since I had been in the seminary and reading the bible. I would try to find other books that talked about the culture of Egypt. I had visited once while I was working in Lebanon, but I only had four days and that was not enough time to see everything. This time I decided to stay for a week. I visited the Cairo Museum where the history of the dynasties was on display. I also took a day trip to see the pyramids of Giza. While there I took the opportunity to take a camel ride. Next, I went to Luxor to see the most splendid Egyptian temples. I then travelled the next three days on the Nile. We cruised from Luxor to Abu Simbel on a boat named "Cleopatra". In Abu Simbel I visited the temple of Ramses. From there I travelled back to Cairo and then on to Tel Aviv.

I went to Jerusalem to see all the religious sites. I visited the famous Wailing Wall, The Dome of the Rock, The Church of the Nativity, and the site of Jesus's Baptism. I also walked the Via Dolorosa to the Tomb of Jesus. I was able to visit the Dead Sea and Jericho.

When I returned from my trip, I received a call from Phil Osterman. I had met him years before when he directed Let My People Come. He had wanted me to work on that project, but I was travelling and had to turn it down. He was calling to ask me to work on his new project, Strip, at the Village Gate.

I accepted the role and after a few weeks of rehearsal, Mr. Osterman received a call that our Producer, Michael Bennett, had passed away. When we opened the show, Mr. Osterman had asked Mike Nichols to see the show and possibly back it. Mr. Nichols was not interested. The only other possibility for Mr. Osterman at the time was to ask me to "come out" as a sex change. I had no desire to do that and it was no guarantee of success. After two weeks the show closed, but I felt that it was a good show and the cast was very disappointed.

My good friend, Felix De Masi, decided to close his atelier. He was going to work from home and only for his close friends. I went to visit him and he told me that he was tired and not feeling well. I tried to call him a couple of days later and he did not answer. Felix finally returned my call and explained that he had been in the Roosevelt Hospital. On one of my visits with him, he confessed that he had been diagnosed with AIDS. He was taking the medicine, but it made him feel bad because it attacked his nerves. A few weeks later he was again admitted to the hospital. Felix's good friends, Leola Harlow, Beverly Spirit, and I went to visit him. That evening he was in very good spirits. We were making plans to all have dinner when he got out of the hospital. The nurse even let us stay an extra hour. We left him at 9 p.m. Felix De Masi passed away at 1:20 the following morning. I had lost a lot of people I knew to this disease but losing Felix really affected me.

Bobby and I continued our relationship as it had been, enjoying dinners, shows, and special occasions with his family. I asked him again about buying a condo in Manhattan and once again he thought I was too stressed and wanted to send me on a vacation. Once again, I would travel alone. This time I went to Argentina. I wanted to go where one of my favorite styles of music was born. The Argentine tango was originated in the bordellos of Buenos Aires. It was forbidden to be played on the radio or danced in society. It wasn't until approximately 1920 when the Parisians started dancing the Tango in Europe and Hollywood used it in movies like Sunset Boulevard, that it became socially acceptable in Argentina. The other reason I wanted to go to Buenos Aires was to bring flowers to the tomb of Eva Peron. I admired her very much and was also happy to be able to acquire a signed copy of her autobiography, "La Razon De Mi Vida".

My life continued with the same routine. I worked club dates around New York, spent time with Bobby and continued to take care of my mother. Mercedes and Enrique had sold their business and moved to Ft. Lauderdale, so I had to take care of my mother all by myself. On Sundays, I would frequently visit my friend Ralf Ferrer aka Nefertiti. He would always have a couple of guests and we'd have drinks and reminisce about good times and our friends. More recently the subject was how we had lost so many of those friends. One of those Sundays, Ralf told me that he was going to need me to take care of his new exotic bobcat because the doctor was admitting him to the hospital. He told me he had a virus. Ralf said she needed to be fed six cans of tuna fish and a package of raw chicken gizzards daily. He gave me the phone number of his father and aunt in Puerto Rico and asked me to call them if he became sick. He also gave me the number of an exotic animal sanctuary in Georgia that I was also to call. He had already made arrangements with them to take Daisy. He told me that if something happened to him that I could have anything I wanted from the apartment and to give the keys to the building superintendent.

I went to see him in the hospital a few days later and his health was declining. He was still able to have conversations and he informed the hospital staff that if they needed to discuss anything with someone that they were to discuss it with me. A few days later, I received a

188

call from the hospital telling me that he had gone into a coma. When I spoke with the doctor, he told me that Ralf only had about a week to live. I immediately called his family and explained the situation to them. I also called the sanctuary and asked them to come and get Daisy. When they arrived in New York, they called me to meet them at the apartment. They tranquilized Daisy so she could fly to her new home in Georgia. Nefertiti went to heaven.

My mother became ill and her doctor sent her to the Holy Name Hospital in Teaneck, NJ. She was very sick for a few weeks. And I would go to sit with her every evening. Her health had been declining with each passing day. Her doctor called me around 3 a.m. on February 12, 1992 to tell me that my mother had passed. I had already made cremation arrangements for my mother so at this emotional time I only had to call the funeral home. It would take two weeks to receive her ashes and I began to make plans to take her back to Spain.

I contacted my friend Mara and she offered to have me stay with her in Seville. I had planned on spreading my mother's ashes around the area of the city where she had been born. A friend of Mara, Valentino, took me to see a bird sanctuary in the village of Jovellanos. I decided to spread my mother's ashes there in this beautiful place.

When I returned from Spain, Hanns Wolters called me to tell me that Martin Charnin was asking for me to be in a benefit show that Tony Randall was doing for the Actor's Studio. Mr. Wolters asked that I receive $250 even though it was a benefit. The show was to be held at the Roseland Dance Hall in New York City. It was to star Tony Randall and Jack Klugman. The show was also to feature many celebrities such as Beverly Sills, Tyne Daly and Petula Clark.

I met with Tony and Jack at the Rainbow Room. Tony explained his concept of what he saw for me. He was going to come out singing "Red Sails in the Sunset". While he was singing, he wanted me to come out behind him and do a strip tease. The audience would get a laugh and I would steal the show. The table price to attend was $25,000. The show was such a success that they called me again a few months later to reprise my role when they put the show on at the Lyceum Theatre.

My relationship with Bobby was still as it had been. I was now alone since my mother had passed away. I was getting older and was beginning to worry about my future. I really needed him to understand that I needed more security than a fancy dinner and bottle of champagne or beautiful clothes. I told Bobby that he either needed to provide me financial security or provide me a place to live. I was very concerned as to what would happen to me if anything happened to him. He was sixteen years older than me and was suffering from heart disease. His response was, "Aren't I paying the rent?" I told him that was only for the present, I needed something substantial for the future. After hearing his response, I knew there was no point discussing it anymore. It had been six years and he still didn't understand or want to.

I wrote a letter to my agent in Austria, Eberhard Angenendt. I told him that if he could get me booked in the cabarets, I was interested. He told me that he had plenty of work for me in Austria and Germany. I reminded him that I was now 52 years old but assured him that I looked more like 40. I sent him some photographs and he sent me a contract.

I called Bobby and gave him an ultimatum. I told him that I loved him, but I needed him to buy me the condo or I was accepting contracts to go to work in Europe so that I could buy it myself. His answer was, "Let's have dinner tomorrow." At dinner, I mentioned that there were some condos for sale near Wall Street for only $98,000. I told him that if he cared for me that he would come through for me on this. He said that his money was tied up in stocks and that he didn't want to change any of his financials to buy a condo and that as long as he was around, I wouldn't have anything to worry about. I told
190

him, "That's exactly what I worry about. How long you will be around."

It was time to go to Germany. I called Bobby from the Kennedy airport and told him that I wouldn't be back for a while. I told him I packed my costumes and was taking the contracts in Europe. Bobby started to cry and offered me $10,000 not to leave. I thanked him for everything he had done for me and I hung up the phone.

Chapter 22 – On the Road Again

My first contract was in a cabaret: Red Apple in a town called Lorrach which was on the border next to Basel, Switzerland. This was the beginning of working with Eberhard in Austria and Germany. After a few months, Eberhard sent me back to Zurich where I was very well known. However, the large cabarets where I had worked no longer existed. I was booked in St. Pauli Bar. When I was working in the Maxim and La Puce and all the other cabarets, there would have been absolutely no way that I would have ever worked at the St. Pauli. To my surprise, the St. Pauli was now "the club" to be in. It was a very local oriented place where you only heard people speaking Zurich Dutch, which is the dialect of Zurich as each region of Switzerland has their own dialect. Not even those who spoke high German understood Zurich Dutch.

After my time at the St. Pauli, I was booked into other parts of Switzerland where I had never been before. These were all mostly small clubs as the wonderful and exciting cabarets were all gone now.

I rented a studio in Zurich on Roland Strasse number 27 studio 8. Having this place allowed me to keep my extra luggage and be able to spend my days off. I had a friendship with a Swiss man, Andreas Huber. Whenever I had a day off in whatever small town I was working in, I would take the train back to Zurich to have dinner and go out partying with Andreas. We took a trip to Florida so that I could visit with my sister, Mercedes. While we were there, he asked me to marry him. So, I accepted, and we married on July 18, 1994 while visiting Florida. When I returned to Switzerland, I immediately received my resident permit. I was now able to live and work as a Swiss native.

In April 1993, I flew to Seville to visit my friend Mara and to attend the Sevilla Fair. This fair celebrates the city and the history of Flamenco. People attend the fair dressed in the traditional clothing from their regions. There were parades of hundreds of years old carriages and beautiful Andalusian horses with ladies dressed in their folk outfits full of gorgeous ruffles. Lola Flores, one of the most famous Flamenco artists and hostess of the fair for 25 years, invited us to her tent. Her tent is the one that would be televised as it had a large stage that would play host to the most prominent singers and musicians. One of the singers in the show was Paquita Rico, considered the most beautiful face of the Spanish screen. It was an unforgettable evening.

Being married to Andreas was easy. He was a very easy man to be with. I moved into Andreas's place on Gothard Strasse in Zurich. I got along very well with all his friends and so now I was moving in a very different circle of people. Our friends were professional people from different walks of Swiss life. I would travel whenever I wanted without any problem from Andreas. We never argued about anything. I could travel or stay home or whatever I wanted, and Andreas was fine with it. We enjoyed each other's company when we were together and were each on our own when we were apart. I was now getting older and work was getting harder and harder to come by. So, in 1998 I decided to return to my place in Ft. Lauderdale and retire. My separation with Andreas was mutual. There was no trouble or hard feelings between us. He told me he hated to see me leave but if that's what I wanted to do then it was okay with him. I came home on December 18, 1998.

Living in Ft. Lauderdale was nice. I lived close to the ocean and my favorite sister. I was able to build a better relationship with my niece and nephew and was happy to have my family close by.

Through a mutual friend, Bobby found out that I was back in the United States and living in Ft. Lauderdale. He called me and we renewed our friendship. Once again, he called me every day and would come and visit. Bobby liked my place and enjoyed Ft. Lauderdale as it was a new place for him. He also offered to help me with anything I needed and would be there for me. My life felt complete. I had Bobby and my family. Until the ugly day on September 19, 1999 when my sister tragically died.

After her death I went into a deep depression. I not only lost my sister but had to watch how much this event was destroying my niece and nephew. Andreas came to see me and asked me to return to Switzerland. I went back to visit for a few weeks, and we took a vacation in Rome. I just felt lost. I then went to visit Mara in Seville. I was contemplating a permanent move there. However, in 2002 Mara became ill and passed away. After that I lost all illusions of ever living in Spain.

Bobby's mother passed away but he told me he was too old to marry now. My long-distance relationship with Bobby was good, but I was just not happy with my own life at the time. I had a friend who lived in Las Vegas. I hadn't seen her in over twenty years, but she got my number from a mutual friend, Veronica Lewis, and began to call me weekly. During each conversation she would say the same thing, "I love you like a sister." She kept on me to move to Las Vegas, but she had let me down too many times in the past. At first, I had mixed emotions about moving, but I was not happy in Ft. Lauderdale, so I decided to put my condo up for sale.

I moved to Las Vegas on October 22, 2004. While living here, I decided to give a call to Dixie Evans. Dixie Evans was a friend of mine who was a burlesque feature. I had known her for years and we had kept in touch. Dixie was living in Helendale, California where she was helping to take care of "Exotic World" after its creator, Jennie Lee had passed. She was happy to hear from me and told me that because I now lived in Vegas, I had no more excuses and that I had to come to her stripper's reunion that next summer and do a show on Legends' Night. That year at New Years, Bobby came to visit me and stayed for a month. He was very happy with my choice to move to Las Vegas.

At the beginning of the new year, I began my search for a cardiologist. When I was still living in Florida, I had been diagnosed with Bradycardia. Bradycardia is a disease of the heart wherein the heart beats at a very low rate. There is no medicine to treat it and no cure. It can only be treated with a pacemaker. My heart was beating at 40 beats per minute. At that rate I was told it was still safe providing it didn't go below that. I found a very good cardiologist, Dr. Allan Stahl. He told me that I would need to see him every six months and had me checking my pulse daily. He said that if I ever went below 40 beats, I would need to see him immediately to schedule getting a pacemaker.

That April, Luke Littell called me as Dixie had told him that I would be coming to the reunion and would be performing. He wanted to let me know that they were going to hold the Friday Night Legends' show at the Holiday Inn in Helendale. He told me he would take care of the hotel for me and I confirmed that I would be there to do the show.

On June 3rd, I drove to Helendale, CA with my pet, Linda. I checked into the Holiday Inn and got dressed to join everyone for the cocktail hour. I saw so many people that I had known from the old days with whom I had worked. I also met for the first time some of the new burlesque performers. This was when I met Dirty Martini, Indigo Blue, Paula Sjunneson "The Swedish Housewife", and World Famous Bob. That evening I made my return to Burlesque. When I took the stage, in the front row sat Tempest Storm and Liz Renay. I performed to a great audience and afterward talked with Dixie and saw Camille 2000 for the first time in 20 years. I was with Kiva who was my co-feature during the good years working in the Ohio circuit.

When I awoke the next morning, I had no energy. I knew that it was due to my heart. I asked if the front desk had any means of helping me check my pulse rate. It was in the thirties. I realized that I was not going to be able to go to the ranch in the hot sun. I gave Dixie my apologies and left for Vegas. I stopped in every service area and had some black coffee. When I finally got home, I called Dr.

196

Stahl and left a message. Within a few hours the nurse returned my call and told me to be at the office at 8 a.m. Monday morning. When they took my vitals at the office, my pulse was 37. Dr. Stahl arranged for me to have my pacemaker implanted at the Summerlin Hospital on June 15th, 2005. I called my dear friend here in Vegas with the news and she said, "I will drive you to the hospital if the procedure is on a Monday which is our day off, but that's all I can do for you." I needed someone to be there for me for at least a week, so I called my dear friend Laura Moreno to come from New Jersey and help me. The implantation of a pacemaker carries with it one possible negative outcome and that is the possibility that the patient's heart will stop. It was during my recovery from this very scary and dramatic procedure that my friend who "loves me like a sister", let me down one more time.

Learning to live life with a pacemaker meant I had to focus on simple things that most people never think about. I couldn't use my cell phone on the left side and had to keep it away from me even on the right. I couldn't be near generators or even near a car with the motor running while the hood is up. I had to learn to be careful at security in the airports. Just random things that most people never have to give a second thought to. I also always had to concern myself with covering the scar when wearing anything strapless or low cut. I was also fearful of crowds, because if I were to get hit in the area of the pacemaker it could stop. It was very traumatic learning how to live with a pacemaker. My life changed a lot but it was for the best because I finally had some energy again.

My relationship with Bobby continued as it had. We would talk every day, and he would visit me frequently. Bobby sent me on a trip to Spain to see my sisters and we had a lovely visit. It was wonderful to be able to spend two months with them.

In 2006 Dixie Evans moved to Las Vegas. That year they held "Miss Exotic World" in Las Vegas for the first time at the Celebrity Theatre. The reunion was fabulous. I had a great time with Tura Satana and Ricci Cortez.

I had my last contract in 1997 so the year before was my first performance since then. I was glad that I had kept some of my costumes. Since 2005 I have been known in the community as a Legend. The Burlesque Hall of Fame, formerly Exotic World, has given performers like me the opportunity to not be forgotten. It has allowed those of us who spent our lives in the theatres and clubs to be able to share with the neo-burlesque movement our history and the details of what it was like to work in the world of burlesque. That is what Jennie Lee had intended with her museum and we continue that tradition of sharing today.

When I am booked in a burlesque festival, I am often asked to teach a class. Most of the time they want to hear from me what it was like in my day. The young people find most fascinating that it was a job and it was hard work. It wasn't just wearing a gown and wigs and feathers, we worked 12-hour days. There was a lot of competition and jealousy between dancers which was unnecessary because at that time there was work for everyone. I can remember clients telling me what other dancers would gossip about while I was on stage performing. I even experienced other dancers telling club owners not to hire me and arriving only to find out that my contract had been cancelled. I also had to experience club owners staring very closely at first meeting because they had been told that I had many surgeries. Once they saw me they said they were going to tell the other dancer that she should visit my doctor. Club owners frequently wanted to go to bed with you. That was a constant battle. In those days you were often treated like a criminal. Landlords wouldn't rent to you if they knew what you did for work. Local law enforcement elections were always a dangerous time, because the police would do multiple raids just to make it look good to the public.

I was still spending time with Bobby occasionally when he would visit. He visited me in the spring of 2007. Bobby's favorite Las Vegas show was Folies Bergere. He loved seeing the dancers perform the can can and always wanted to go see it when he visited. Bobby and I loved to go to shows and spend time drinking French champagne and having wonderful dinners at all the different hotels. We also spent a few days in Reno.

The day he returned to New York, we talked about taking a trip out of the country for the first time together. I had told him about Acapulco, and we were making plans to go the following January.

On the evening of the 21st of December, we had a long conversation on the phone. Bobby seemed to be well and acted like his usual self. The following day, I received a phone call from his brother, Richard, informing me that Bobby had suffered a massive stroke. I couldn't believe it. I asked what the diagnosis was, and his brother told me that they had him on life support.

I began to make plans for an immediate flight to New York. Richard was always at the hospital so his wife, Gloria, was keeping me informed. My flight was scheduled to fly into Brooklyn on the 27th. The morning of the 26th, Richard called to tell me that Bobby had passed. He was 80 years old.

Even though I could have stayed in Brooklyn with Bobby's family, I decided to stay in New Jersey with my friend, Laura Moreno. I rented a car so that we could drive into Brooklyn. The first day of the wake, I noticed that Aldo Frustaci, Bobby's lawyer, wasn't there. I went to see him to let him know that Bobby had passed. He had not been informed. It was then that he handed me a copy of Bobby's will. To my surprise, Bobby had failed me. He always told me that he would take care of me even after his death. That was not the case. Even though I was in the will, I was very disappointed with the content. He had made the will when I was living in Switzerland and had never changed it.

My life became very sad and lonely after Bobby's death. I made the decision to not have a relationship with anyone after Bobby. I missed him for many years and continue to do so because he was a wonderful man who always treated me well. At the time I had a beautiful Maltese named,

Linda. She had been a gift to me from Bobby. She got sick in 2009 and I had to put her to sleep. It really broke my heart. I cried over the loss of her for many months until in 2010 when I got my little Maltese, Maja. She has been my companion ever since.

Today, I live a very quiet life, with Maja. I am currently fighting squamous cell carcinoma. I received seven weeks of radiation treatment, after which I had to wait three months for my follow up PET Scan. The scan showed that the radiation killed the carcinoma but they found a new growth in one of my lymph nodes. I underwent surgery to have it removed and will spend the summer of 2020 receiving chemotherapy through a surgically placed port. My doctors are very optimistic and with my trust in them and my faith in God, I will beat it too.

For the very first time I have begun going back and reflecting on what has been my life. When I meditate on it, I see what I have lived and done, my happy days, my love for life, the men that I have loved, the love of my mother and sisters and family and friends. I commune with God daily and have come to the decision that if I could live my life again, I wouldn't change anything. I would live exactly as I have. I think about myself as that child in Cuba who was insulted and abused, and then about all the places that Burlesque took me, I can't imagine my life being any better than my journey from Havana to Burlesque. It's been a great polyfacetic life. It has been full of emotion, pain and suffering, but I find myself at peace. My faith has always been a big part of my life and I still find comfort in it now. If I ask myself, "Do you have anyone to blame?" The answer is "No." I feel we all have a destiny, and this has been mine.

Acknowledgements

I would like to thank Lily Star for her tenacity and her dedication to this project and to Scott Ewalt for contributing his many talents to this book along with his much appreciated advice. It is because of their love and support that I am able to share my story.

Much love and gratitude to Dr. Lucky for also being a source of support and knowledge, and for working so diligently with Julie Rackow to create my funding campaign video.

Thank you to Lolita Haze, who photographed my portraits, Julie Mist and Tim McCarthy for their friendship and publishing advice, Jo Wheldon for sharing her knowledge and for her guidance, Molly Boom Boom for proofreading, Brian Gressley and Blanche DeBris for their positive and helpful feedback and to Susie Cardee and Sylvia Rivera for their lifelong friendship, support, and love.

Thank you to J. D. Doyle for the archival images of the Powderpuff Revue and to Ed Barnes and Derek Jackson for their Burlesque Hall of Fame photographs.

I would also like to extend my gratitude to those who contributed to my funding campaign. Without their support this project would not have been possible.

Author Biographies

Lily Star is a theatrical performer turned burly girl. She has over 30 years of experience as a dancer, instructor and choreographer. Lily has staged theatrical productions and dance numbers for students ranging from grade school to college, for multiple theatre production companies and for the Las Vegas Golden Rainbow. She has also created production numbers at the Burlesque Hall of Fame Weekender. In 2019, Lily was chosen to be a mentor for the Golden Legend Champion Challenge. She performs with Burlesque legends, Tiffany Carter and Lovey Goldmine. Lily is a graduate of Elon University and currently resides in Las Vegas.

Scott Ewalt is an artist, burlesque historian and archivist. He received the Sassy Lassy award from the Burlesque Hall of Fame in 2013 for his contribution to the legends of burlesque. He has worked with Marinka as well as Liz Renay, Kitten Natividad, Tura Satana, Haji, Tempest Storm and April March. He lives in New York City.

www.ingramcontent.com/pod-product-compliance
Lightning Source LLC
Chambersburg PA
CBHW041930260326
41914CB00009B/1248